D1368209

Fact
and
Comment

Fact
and
Comment

Malcolm S. Forbes

 Alfred A. Knopf   New York   1974

THIS IS A BORZOI BOOK
PUBLISHED BY ALFRED A. KNOPF, INC.

Published in the United States by Alfred A. Knopf, Inc., New York,
and simultaneously in Canada by Random House of Canada Limited,
Toronto.
Distributed by Random House, Inc., New York.

Grateful acknowledgment is made to Charterhouse Books, Inc.,
for permission to reprint "Malcolm Forbes" from *Good Times: An Oral
History of America in the Nineteen Sixties*, copyright © 1973 by
Peter Joseph.

Library of Congress Cataloging in Publication Data:

Forbes, Malcolm S., date.
  Fact and comment.
  Editorials from Forbes magazine.
    1. Business—Addresses, essays, lectures.
2. Success—Addresses, essays, lectures. 3.   Editorial.
I. Title.
HF5011.F67 1974 388 73–20737
ISBN 0–394–49187–4

Manufactured in the United States of America
First Edition

To STEVE FORBES:

"Jr." in a genealogical sense but "senior" in thinking and third generation to be writing "Fact and Comment" in *Forbes* magazine.

Contents

Foreword

Through sheer ability (spelled i-n-h-e-r-i-t-a-n-c-e) I have become Editor-in-Chief of *Forbes* magazine and President of Forbes, Inc., which at the moment includes a couple of profitable subsidiaries leavened by a couple of unprofitable ones. Far-flung we are in a geographical sense; far-flung we ain't in a big, conglomerate sense.

Since my late father, B. C. Forbes, published the first issue of the magazine that bears his name on September 15, 1917, the lead-off feature in every one of the issues has been the opinionated observations of its editors under the heading of "Fact and Comment."

Ninety-nine percent of these editorials for the past fifty-six years have been written by Forbeses. Shortly after coming to work for *Forbes* following a Purple Hearted discharge from the U.S. Army in August, 1945 (contrary to occasional reader accusation, the wound was in the leg and not the head), Dad had me write one editorial per issue, which appeared on his "Fact and Comment" pages, with my name under it. Now I do the same with my son, Steve—M. S. Forbes, Jr.

The ones in this volume, though, are entirely of my own doing. Writing these editorials is the most fun and least work part of managing the magazine.

It wasn't always thus, though.

When Dad, in the Scottish burr he never lost, first told me I was to write one for each issue, I was both excited and worried. "Keep them short, terse, to the point," he instructed me. "Say what you want with brevity and leave palavering to others." Although *Forbes* appears but twice a month, it seemed to me that the due date of my editorial contribution occurred far more frequently. I'd stew over and chew over what the subject matter should be and draft, redraft, and abandon several subjects before finally appearing in my father's office with the result.

He was a tolerant if tough man, and literally never changed my written thought. He used an incisive editing pencil, and simply sharpened—mostly by crossing out words —what I had wrought. One of my earliest efforts (page 180 herein) suggested that the National Association of

Manufacturers should drop dead. This advice shocked their membership considerably more than my father; he ran it as written, although he didn't share the view. Letters to the editor were not in short supply for several weeks thereafter.

As time went on, the struggle to write editorials became much less of a struggle. I guess it was a combination of things, beginning with a realization that what I wrote didn't necessarily have worldwide reverberations. As a matter of fact, with rare exception it was hard to detect so much as a tremor even from our subscribers. Too, I began having more and more opinions about more and more, and unconsciously I had discovered the commentator's secret weapon—that so long as you can wield words, it isn't necessarily necessary to know what you're talking about.

Thus, following Dad's death twenty years ago, writing all of "Fact and Comment" wasn't difficult. With an interest in almost anything interesting, accompanied by a stupendous lack of knowledge about many of the subjects, I enjoy pontificating about everything under the sun and beyond.

It is really quite an extraordinary privilege—and one which I have enjoyed abusing these many years—to be able to write what I will and have it untouched by the wiser men and abler editors who abound at *Forbes* magazine.

That's the most appealing advantage of being a sole proprietor of a periodical. When occasionally we've been urged to go public with Forbes, Inc. stock, or been tempted to undertake expansion that was beyond our in-house resources, I have firmly, unequivocably, said nay. "In my lifetime we'll never grow so big that we can't afford to stay private" is the Napoleonic way this sole *Forbes* shareholder phrases it. I usually manage to rustle up a few ostensibly sensible reasons—but the real one is here, in this book: the fun of being able to have and express opinions uninhibited by facts or the Boss.

I'm it, and heartily recommend the job.

MALCOLM S. FORBES

January 31, 1974

A Note
from the Compiler

Editorials are usually written on matters of the moment. When moment and matter pass, so does an editorial's relevance. There are, though, three types that can live longer than yesterday's headlines.

One category, of course, is on matters that still matter. Politics, the stock market, transportation, energy, ecology would all qualify—at least when this book was put together.

A second type that may live is the editorial that was emphatically right or—more fun—emphatically wrong about a major issue, event, or person. Hence the chapters "Prophecies Fulfilled . . ." and ". . . And Prophecies Unfulfilled."

Finally, there are the comments that are not pegged to the daily news. Such are the editorials in the chapters on family, food, human nature, and youth and aging.

Because my father has opined on so many subjects, many of his observations defied convenient classification, or more accurately, chapterization. With these, the easy way was taken: They are lumped together in the chapters "Tilting Windmills" and "Observations—On Target."

A note of caution-*cum*-candor: Such a compilation as this cannot be read at one sitting. Only an insomniac or malicious book reviewer could or would do that. Rather, like wine, you should take this book in sips. Whether it is vintage or vinegar is for you to decide.

M. S. FORBES, JR.

Fact
and
Comment

Thoughts on the Art of My Craft

Occasionally, someone asks me, "Do you really write the editorials under 'Fact and Comment' in *Forbes* magazine?"

I like to assume a compliment is intended, although from the tone of voice or the tenor of letter it's often painfully plain that the querier is expressing incredulity that anyone could write such stuff.

Actually, writing these editorials is the most thoroughly pleasurable privilege of this man's job. Here, I can express big fat opinions often derived from a modicum of facts and seldom inhibited by the latter.

Yes, I have the fun of writing 'em, and you, poor reader, can suffer—or ignore—'em.

11/1/71

It tickles me no end when people get ticked off at those of us who comment audibly and in print on events and problems.

I've never yet come across one for which I or my brethren in the pundit business haven't got answers. That's what we're paid for.

Why clutter up your full or empty mind with a bunch of facts that might inhibit the solve-ability of us who must express an opinion? After all, all the world cries out for a solution to its problems, and we supply them right and left. (Some in high places think more left than right, of course.)

Come to think of it, it's we who should be giving our deplorers and detractors the blast, because 99 percent of the time they don't do as we say.

You'd think those in positions of responsibility were constrained by the facts and dimensions of the problems they're in charge of. But is that a good reason to tee off on those of us who know all the answers and provide them at relatively small cost?

12/15/69

It is a widely accepted axiom that it is generally a good idea to know what you are talking about, if you must talk about it. Recently, I had this elementary lesson retaught.

While visiting in Bermuda, my wife and I were invited to dinner by Mr. and Mrs. Robert F. Black. He heads

Cleveland's White Motor Company. All was proceeding most amicably until the writer asked his host a question: "I'm sure you don't like to speak disparagingly of a competitor, but I'd be interested in knowing what you frankly think of Reo's new truck motor cab—the one where the whole cab lifts off to get at the engine."

A sound Dale Carnegie approach, I thought—talking in terms of Mr. Black's interests—and I was curious about this new idea. It turned out I was certainly talking about something that interested him.

"Speak *disparagingly* about it!" Mr. Black exploded. "The new cab that Reo makes!" At this point his face was somewhat red.

"I *personally* have spent five years perfecting that development. It's the biggest forward move in the whole trucking business . . . and *White* Motor Company has spent $2 million advertising it—and you attribute it to *Reo!*"

Lamely attempting to restore peace, I tried a light note. "Er-a-ha-ha, maybe you didn't advertise it in the right mediums, like *Forbes*, for instance, ha-ha."

Ha-ha.

On the way home my wife turned to me and suggested, ever so gently, "Dear, if you must talk, next time, as a favor to me, will you know what you're talking about?"

9/1/51

Much of the difference between "straight" reporting, as theoretically exemplified in newspaper articles, and "interpretive" reporting, as presumably exemplified in such publications as *Forbes*, lies in the latter's sparing but vigorous use of adjectives and constant use of active verbs rather than passive ones. For readers to read intelligently it is important to be aware of this.

Not wary of it, just aware of it.

Look what you can do with words—

If the company had a bad year, but the president expresses optimism, the interpretive reporter, depending on his knowledge and point of view, could describe the president's optimism in two ways. "Despite last year's poor showing, Chairman Smith was full of promises for the coming year, claiming things would be better"—which sounds like shallow optimism and a refusal to face facts. On the other hand, "Chairman Smith frankly accepted the blame for last year's earnings decline and outlined the steps already taken and others planned to ensure increased profits for the year ahead," sounds as though Smith faced the facts, everything is under control.

If Mr. Smith dealt humorously in some replies to perhaps foolish questions from stockholders on the floor, he could be described as "having brushed off worried stockholders' questions with quips and jokes." Reader reaction? Mr. Smith doesn't take losses and stockholders seriously. A jokester. Or on the other hand, "Mr. Smith handled even *frivolous* questions from the floor with *patient* good humor." Quite a different picture of the same incident.

Or consider this situation. A straight newspaper account might report that Chairman Smith "attended the meeting." But an interpretive report could have him "striding in and firmly taking control of the meeting"—if the impression he made was a favorable one. If it was unfavorable, he might be described as "sitting slumped in his chair, impatiently brushing aside persistent stockholder questions." Only a few words involved in either case, but what a difference in the impression conveyed!

Is interpretive writing wrong? Is objective reporting preferable? Of course not. If Mr. Smith is self-satisfied and shallowly optimistic and has lost the drive that built his company and brought him up the ladder, then the investor ought to know it. An adjective-less, neutral-verbish recitation of the "facts" of the meeting would be of only limited use to the investor looking for meaningful interpretation.

If, on the other hand, Mr. Smith is an able man whose industry and company hit serious problems but tackled them with great prospects for success, the investor should know that. Merely looking at the figures in terms of an earnings decline might cause him to sell when he shouldn't.

As Jack Webb used to say on "Dragnet," "just the facts" are quite essential. But to the intelligent investor and business-man, so are interpretations.

1/15/63

Two of the all too many pitfalls facing those of us who pontificate in print year after year are being repetitious and/or contradictory.

A little over four years ago Florida's then-Governor Claude Kirk, Jr., was engaged in assorted headline-making antics, apparently seeking to attract attention as a Republican vice-presidential possibility on the Nixon ticket. This prompted me to write a succinct editorial, which appeared in the January 1, 1968, *Forbes*:

GOVERNOR KIRK
Jerk.

Four and a half years later, in *Forbes* (August 15, 1972), I concluded "Fact and Comment" with this editorial:

MIRRORS
People who think people are jerks are.

Yep, you guessed it—I received the following letter on stationery of Kirk and Co., signed by Claude R. Kirk, Jr:

It is particularly annoying to me to correspond with someone I do not know . . . who I don't want to know . . . who
has made a comment about me . . . not knowing me!

However, I note that you finally have realized your
own personal shortcomings, and/or description, and I'm
happy to see your confession in print.

11/1/72

Writing is a funny business, being of course no "business"
at all. A rare few make money at it—such as the fluent ones
who ghostwrite papers of state for presidents and prime
ministers and the like; advertising copywriters who make
mints on phrases about Twins, Toni, and relief being just a
swallow away; the brilliant, prideless prolific ones who turn
out scripts for movies or TV serials.

But real writers—that is, capital W Writers—rarely
make much money. Their biggest reward is the occasional
reader's response. It couldn't matter less to a Writer if the
reaction is favorable or unfavorable.

Commentors in print voicing big fat opinions—you
might call us small w writers—get considerably more feed-
back than Writers.

The measure of how much reader response means was
perhaps never more poignantly expressed than in the following letter by Woodrow Wilson:

Princeton, New Jersey
23 October, 1898

Mr. Barton A. Konkle,
Philadelphia, Pa.,

My dear Sir,

It is certainly one of the rewards of authorship to get such
a letter as yours of last Thursday. I am so far from regarding it
as an intrusion that I wish to thank you for it most heartily.

A writer of course never sees his audience; he does not know how many he is reaching or in what way he is being regarded by his readers. He must keep heart amidst the embarrassing silence, and try to believe that what he writes is at any rate worth saying and deserving of an audience, for the sake of the truth or the cheer or the right moral impulse, or the mere human interest, that is in it. It's a lonely business at best. Your letter comes to me pitched in so genuine a key of friendliness and appreciation that I must accept it not only with pleasure but also with gratitude. It heartens me and touches me very near the quick.

With sincere appreciation,

Very cordially yours,
Woodrow Wilson

10/1/66

Advice from and to the Top

ONCE IN A WHILE

There's wisdom in recognizing that the Boss is.

1/15/71

After working in an office for many and many a year, I remain more firmly convinced than ever that the most useful piece of equipment in it remains the scrap basket.

10/1/67

Some of the biggest bores I've ever known are men who have been highly successful in business, particularly some self-made heads of big companies.

Before the first olive has settled into the first martini, they pour the stories of their lives into the nearest and sometimes the remotest ears capturable. If it's at dinner, by the time you've had a third telling along with the third course, you're anesthetized, if lucky, or ready to run, not walk, to the nearest exit.

These men have indeed paid the price of success. To rise to the top of a big company often takes a totality of effort, concentration, dedication.

Others, too, have to pay part of the price. Wife and children are out of mind even when in sight, subject to fitful gusts of affection and more frequent outpourings of the things that money can buy. There is no time for friends unconnected with the business at hand.

There is also danger to others in the success of this type. Having "made good" in the world of business, surrounded at the office and elsewhere by the duly Respectful, Worshipful, and Dependent, our Man at the Top often comes to think that his opinions on all matters are as important as those made at his desk.

I will never forget how shocked I was as a young man to hear some of the comments on national and world affairs made by one of the most important businessmen in this country at that time. His was a name spoken with reverence on Wall Street and on Main Streets everywhere. He knew his business, the biggest of its kind in the world, inside out. But he had everything else he talked about upside down. At dinner with my father one night in 1938, I heard some of his observations. Hitler? Straightening out Germany and fixing the Reds. Roosevelt? Somebody ought to have shot that S.O.B. years ago. League of Nations? An international conspiracy to involve this country in Europe's old quarrels. Unions? Comment unprintable. These were the opinions of a man who headed for two decades a company employing thousands and whose policies had a major impact on countless other companies.

Fortunately, he was a skinflint and didn't put his money where his mouth was. In Texas today some of the oil-made millionaires do. When their money bags begin bursting at the seams, they are not content to spout oil talk or use the leisure time success has provided them to broaden their own horizons. They promptly want to remake the country and the world in their image. When people and nations don't fit the prejudices born of their ignorance, they promptly want to Birch them into shape.

Does success in business really have to be at the cost of so many and so much? Of course not. And nine out of ten businessmen in America today are proof of the fact.

But, please, save us from the others—both at the dinner table and at the helm of men's affairs.

11/1/61

A vital ingredient of sustained success is occasional failure. Decision making is a prime responsibility of those in top positions, and their batting average between right ones and wrong ones must be high.

Being right most of the time is pretty heady medicine. The higher one is, the less likely are subordinates and associates inclined to argue. Certainly, they are unapt to point out or remind the boss of his boo-boos.

Apparently, it is not a long leap from being right most of the time to the assumption that one is right all the time. At this point there is nothing as essential as an unmistakable mistake of some magnitude to restore the perspective that is needed to ensure continued success.

Joe Louis was long a champion as a result of being up-ended—once—by Max Schmeling. Floyd Patterson came back stronger than ever after Ingemar Johansson gave him a taste of defeat, but no continued appetite for it.

A big shot who has never laid an egg—in his insulated opinion—is in the position of a hen under a similar handicap, about to be made a meal of.

12/15/61

Executives in their thirties and forties are valuable because they're eager and keen and aware of what can, should, needs to be done.

Executives in their fifties and sixties are valuable because they're more relaxed and experienced and often aware of what can't, shouldn't, needn't be done.

8/15/72

All too often we loosely say of a man doing a good job that he is indispensable.

A flattering canard, as so many disillusioned retired and fired have discovered when the world seems to keep on turning without them.

In business a man can come nearest to indispensability by being dispensable in his present job. How can a man move up to new responsibilities if he is the only one able to handle his present tasks? It matters not how small or large the job you now have; if you have trained no one to do it as well, you're not available; you've made your promotion difficult if not impossible.

You may think you've made yourself unfireable, whereas in reality you've made yourself unpromotable.

I can see the heads of all you nabobs bobbing in agreement.

I wonder, though, how many of you can honestly say you have had at least one man able to step into your shoes and do your job as well or possibly better? Try asking today each of the men who report to you for the names of the men under them qualified this very moment to take their job. On their answers you can judge their promotability.

Dispensability precedes indispensability.

1/1/70

Too many corporate employers are too blamed presumptuous in their employment procedures. What earthly right has a prospective employer to require lie detector tests for job applicants? Urinalysis? Fingerprints? Actual and quasi and pseudo psychoanalysis?

It's now mostly illegal for employers to discriminate in hiring on the basis of race, color, creed, and sex preferences.

There are rare exceptions when one thing or the other *may* be relevant to a very particular job. But these instances should be infinitely more rare than present presumptuous practices by many companies.

A day's work for a day's pay is an employer's right to expect.

A day's pay for a day's work is the employee's right to expect.

Getting or giving more by either is an option.

Check your own personnel procedures, and if you're invading a person's privacy, stop it.

Before the courts and the law do.

And before you lose more *good* young people—the able ones are and always will be in short supply.

They think their life is their business and that only the caliber of their work at your business is your business.

12/1/71

For every company of any size the subject of executive retirement presents problems. Most companies make retirement compulsory at a certain age for everyone from president to aged office boy.

It seems to me indisputable that from a stockholder's viewpoint there is great brain waste in any mandatory retirement system. The blanket rule often deprives a company of an executive at the peak of his abilities. No matter what one's previous experience, it takes a bit of time to adjust to the top spot. It is pretty foolish to have to leave just when one is getting the feel of the wheel.

Providing exceptions to a retirement system, of course, is an attempt to square the circle. If discretion is permitted in any way, shape, or form, then the "strong man," who may not be turning out to be the best man, can often bulldoze his way into job perpetuity. Who under him in the corporate structure is about to suggest that in his case no retirement exception is warranted? Forceful presidents are also known to exert a rather substantial influence even on "outside" boards of directors.

. . . Only a compulsory company retirement plan provides a practical answer. As in the armed forces, so too in companies, room at the top must be provided if you are to have able management in depth, to attract and to keep bright, ambitious young men. For it is a matter of sad record that no matter how able, how profitable a management group may be today, that company has only a dim tomorrow if it does not have top replacements in the bull pen, who can do as well or better.

My father used to say that in buying stocks he considered the brains at the helm the most important single factor in his decision. One yardstick he used to measure those brains was whether or not the head man talked with enthusiasm about the man or men immediately under him who could handle the president's job as well or better.

Compulsory executive retirement, often unfair, costly, and inefficient from a stockholder's viewpoint, still appears the only practical answer to a tough problem.

But to apply it at age sixty or even sixty-two is going too far.

10/1/64

Recently, I was sitting around a coffee table with the head men of half a dozen sizable companies. It was a relaxed group en route to a football game.

We got on the subject of boards of directors. There was quite a gamut of opinion as to whether boards in a practical sense were useless or useful.

The chairman of a great and growing merchandising complex has a nineteen-man board, most of the men acquired with the takeover of their companies. They became directors as part of the deal, but he was happy to state they had little to do with directing his direction.

The president–chairman–chief executive officer of a huge, worldwide manufacturing company employing 62,000 said he found his board members quite often individually helpful in terms of advice and judgment on major capital investments, new directions, and so forth. He himself was brought from the ranks by the directors to run the company after it had fallen way behind in its highly competitive industry.

The young founder–runner of a handling outfit with

$40 million in assets said that he had found outside directors and a few outside stockholders such a pain in the neck, such an obstacle to imaginative growth, that he bought out the latter and threw out the former. Now he operates with the legal minimum necessary for a corporate façade.

The president of one of the major transportation systems said he keeps very close to his board, a board that came in as a result of a stockholders' legal battle. If they're out, so's he. It's that simple.

Our discussion grew more animated with every spiked tomato juice, and we covered the angles of outside directors versus inside, of whether there is virtue or not in substantial shareholdings by directors, of large boards versus small, etc.

The discussion consensus seemed to be this:

That in a widely held company the board of directors' greatest contribution is in the selection of the head man and then in keeping out of his hair—until he falls on his face.

That in closely held companies a board of directors as a practical matter is as useless as a hole in the head.

Before all of you proud directors send off irate letters to the publisher of *Forbes*, let me hasten to say that all present agreed there are indeed exceptions, that some directors do make measurable contributions—bank directors, for instance, whose companies keep huge balances, or directors whose companies are huge customers.

But, with the exception of yourself, don't you find most directors do very little directing?

11/15/65

I was with a group of corporate Mighty Moguls, and after a fascinating bit of discussion about executive aircraft and the pros and cons of the exotic ones now available, the subject was turned a bit by the chief executive officer of a building materials outfit doing over half a billion dollars' worth of business yearly.

"I need a jet to get around to our plants and our meetings on the few days I am free to do so.

"It seems to me I spend almost every day in my office doing 'annual' things, like budgets, reports, filings, planning committees, retirement committees, committees of this and that. Every week is full of once-a-year routines.

"Wouldn't it be wonderful if 'annual' meetings could be held and annual reports issued at the president's discretion . . . like every four or five years?"

The presidents present were enchanted, nay, ecstatic at the thought, and their spirits bubbled like a just-popped bottle of Mumm's.

To watch their wistful expressions as the conversation in a few moments returned to reality almost brought a tear to my eye.

10/15/66

I was once starting to write an editorial suggesting that it was about time, if not past time, for companies to issue once again old-fashioned annual reports that were simply that: a couple of pages or so of the figures for the year just past, compared with the previous one. Plain, honest figures, with footnotes designed to enlighten and not obfuscate points that must be made.

I was going to suggest that perhaps stockholders were tired of four-color pictures of pot-bellied corporate presidents and multicolored charts indicating everything is up and up when about all the poor stockholder knows is that his dividends aren't and the P/E ain't.

Then the annual reports started coming across my desk, and I have to admit I've arrived at exactly the opposite conclusion. I *did* find the illustrations and striking presentation of U.S. Industries, for instance, more helpful than bare bones would have been. Just as in *Forbes* we have found showing a man's face is helpful when profiling his accomplishments, I found it interesting to be able to look at the executives who are running U.S. Industries.

So, too, with the AMF report. I had little conception of AMF's enormous diversification in so many exciting leisure-time areas. The bare-bones figures would not have conveyed that visible potential.

It *is* helpful to read what the CEO of a company has to say on the past year, the present year, and his thoughts about his future.

After all, an annual report reports the past. Owners and customers, acquisition prospects and acquisition prospectors, and those who might be called upon for additional finance are all more concerned with a company's today and tomorrow. To evaluate the future, of course, one must be able to study the corporate past performance. But both aspects, the done and the to-be-done, belong in the same package.

So instead of pumping for annual report simplicity as I started out to do, I guess we'll still go for the gussied-up annual report.

5/1/70

Thought for annual report makers:
Sometimes, even accountants agree, it's best to tell the truth.

2/15/72

While there's plenty to be said for doing away with corporate annual meetings, I think that there's more to be said for keeping them.

True, annual meetings are often abused by the asinine

antics of professional publicity seekers. Yet when corporation chiefs must ready themselves annually to face their shareholders, of necessity they must review what's apt to come up, must be ready to answer for shortcomings, ready to outline future prospects, and ready to deal with questions on social problems that don't seem germane to the running of a profitable business. This discipline forces management to think about things it probably otherwise wouldn't.

The fact that often nothing of consequence comes up and only a handful of stockholders show up is quite unimportant next to the beneficial results from management's getting-ready process.

6/15/72

I haven't got a complete solution to this problem—the business of telephoning between busy businessmen.

There are practical aspects to such telephoning.

There are aspects of good manners and politeness in such telephoning.

And for "big shots" who are little men, there are even protocol "problems."

Take the practical side of it. Occasionally, I want to call the president of a big company in connection with an editorial or other matter. The call goes to the company switchboard, thence to his secretary, and then, perhaps, to him. Sometimes there's another layer or two before that. Odds are he will be away on business or in a meeting. (Even if he is in his sauna or taking a snooze, the well-trained executive secretary always describes her boss as in a meeting.)

Since sometimes I, too, am busy—or at least think I am—I ask my secretary to see if she can reach Mr. So-and-So. If the call does succeed in reaching its object, then the fact that he is on the line is relayed back from switchboard to secretary to caller—all of which leaves the party being phoned hanging on for a while for a caller who isn't there.

I have succeeded in solving this problem by asking that if the executive is going to be available, I be brought back on the line before his phone is jingled.

The whole thing is a matter of courtesy and practicality. I am not sure that there's a simple solution.

There are a few who take pride in answering their phone themselves. It's a cinch, though, that they're not in very busy businesses, or there would probably be darned little time left for the executive to do his job.

The final telephone aspect is the protocol bull. You know, the classic case where each big shot wants the other guy to be on the line before he is. These people actually exist. I have sometimes—not frequently—run into one of these twerps. It always dumbfounds me that they are in positions of business prominence.

The last time it happened I was so stunned that such a minnow could be the president of this particular company that I promptly sold my few shares of the stock—on the basis that if this was an example of the company's management, its future was dim.

This whole business-phoning bit isn't a *major* problem, but it *is* a problem.

Solutions anyone?

8/1/65

There's an old axiom in selling to the effect that if you don't ask for the order, you'll never get it.

But asking and receiving are, most times, two very different things.

People *do* like to do business with friends. Making friends is never easy. Making friends of prospects is infinitely harder. The man in the position to sign the order is perhaps ever so faintly aware of what you have in the back of your mind when you invite him to dig divots on your golf club course or to share the sauce at some bar and barbecue.

Be he ever so *en garde*, however, such exposures are infinitely helpful in establishing personal rapport. It's a mighty foolish company that lets the controller make the decisions that should be a sales manager's when it comes to salesmen's expenditures. Quite often the cost of playing golf is as essential to doing business as the cost of the salesman's chair, desk, and telephone.

Entertaining may not always be entertaining, but don't entertain the thought that all business can be done without it.

8/1/66

Every now and again some computa-teer stuck in a city traffic jam figures out how many billions of dollars of working time is wasted waiting for the car ahead to move ahead. The total of such lost productivity is appalling.

Suggested remedies usually involve millions in new highway spending. Occasionally, an imaginative, sensible Barnes [Henry Barnes, longtime New York City Traffic commissioner] appears on the scene and comes up with ways of making much better do with existing facilities.

There is, however, another major time waster that can be cured at no cost: Change the habits of men who keep other men waiting. It is primarily executives who are to blame for this lost time, and it is primarily salesmen—whose efforts make the wheels turn prosperously—that are kept waiting.

Keeping people who have appointments waiting long and often is usually unnecessary. Only a small big shot could think that keeping a salesman cooling his heels is a sign of importance. It's usually a sign of either bad manners or very poor organization on the part of the executive involved. I can think of no one whose job doesn't ultimately depend on selling somebody else something, be it things or services. The customers who waste your salesman's time have to pay for it in the long run, because your upped overhead must ultimately be reflected in the price of what you're selling.

Alert head men once in a while might check the lobbies and waiting rooms of their executive offices. Find out who's been waiting how long for whom.

An able man respects the other fellow's time, the other fellow's job.

If you can't keep appointments, cancel them.

Imagine what a difference in overhead, what a difference in productivity, what a difference in profits would result if half your sales force's waiting time could be turned into calling on additional prospects.

Besides, in the words of an old French proverb, "People count up the faults of those who are keeping them waiting."

3/1/66

It's a rare case indeed when not answering letters is wise. Failure by executives to reply to their mail sows unnecessary ill will that ripples in eddies widely over a long period.

I'm not, of course, talking about form letters, processed and impersonally addressed. I'm talking of a letter addressed to the president or the vice-president in charge of whatnot that contains comments or complaints about a company or its products or its personnel or its policies. It still jolts me to realize that there are many executives in many companies of consequence who are quite indifferent to the treatment accorded their mail—except, of course, letters from big wheels with big orders or those of a personal nature pertaining to contemplated pleasures.

It has often been said—and I have found it to be true—

that much of the need to answer mail disappears with time. If all mail were left for three months before being opened, the passage of time would, in effect, take care of 75 percent to 80 percent of it.

But further analysis, I am sure, would show that the reason much of it no longer needs answering is because it is too late either to fill the order, accept the invitation, or otherwise respond to what prompted the letter in the first place. Sure, the need to answer it has gone, but so has the order, so has the occasion.

Rudeness, a feeling of irritation, of hurt, alone remains. That's good?

I keep a file full of carbons of letters I have written that seem to me to warrant a reply. When the answer arrives, it goes into the file. Periodically, I look the letters over, and it sometimes shocks me to note the names of those who have not replied.

Sometimes, I follow up with a carbon of the first letter and a little memo. Usually, I forget about the matter, but not the person who failed to extend the courtesy of an answer.

It's remarkable, when you think of it, how much plain simple courtesy can do to reap goodwill. If your company or your department or you don't have a mail-answering policy, it's time you sat right down and wrote yourself a suitable directive.

11/15/65

During a conversation with the head of a major company, we got to talking about the volume of mail addressed to corporate presidents.

"Try as I may, I find I just can't answer it all. How do the other fellows do it?" he queried.

From personal experience I could tell him that some

don't. For a man heading an important company to allow letters addressed to him to go unanswered is inexcusable in this day and age.

How can it be done and leave time for the boss to direct the affairs of a company so it is profitable to his stockholders?

First requisite: an intelligent secretary.

She can direct the circulars, printed stuff, and impersonal trivia into the round file. If it's a question or comment about a particular product, a division, service or the lack of it, she can direct it to the appropriate executive for answering.

It's important, though, that the boss does see a reasonable number of complaints and comments. Not just compliments.

There are some very useful shortcuts in replying to letters.

Sometimes, I get very long letters about editorials and articles in *Forbes*. Many of these are answered with two or three words.

If the three-, four-, five-, or six-page letter expresses a compatible point of view, the reply, aside from salutation and signature, consists of two words: "I agree."

If not, the reply, in addition to salutation and signature, is three words: "I don't agree."

Letters of enthusiastic compliments (few) and letters of vehement disagreement (many) also get two-word replies: "Thank you."

The one answer to a letter that remains inadmissible is no answer.

5/1/68

Mussolini used to shake up his visitors by having an office that required a walk of a couple of miles from the door you entered to the desk behind which he sat. Since he ended up hanging upside down in an Italian gas station the long-walk ploy has gone out of fashion for big shots.

There's a more subtle one now, and I find it equally disconcerting: a man sitting behind a desk without a damned thing on it.

It's a pretty cool gimmick, you know. First, it makes the visitor feel inferior, because his own desk is usually a mess, and the conclusion about the Bare Topper must be that he is terribly able and has his work all done, or that he is even smarter and has given it to someone else to do.

I have only come across three of these rare birds, and they do happen to be abler, smarter than most of us—they *do* work, even if the evidence isn't strewn all over their working surfaces.

As an unsuccessful aspirant for the *Daily Princetonian* almost three decades ago, I interviewed RCA's General Sarnoff. Being sufficiently awestruck already by this unique tycoon, I was so wowed by the cleanliness of the desk that I forgot most of my questions and had to write the interview mostly about the fact that an empty desk top didn't necessarily imply an empty mind behind it.

Number two on this short list is Bill Grace, who has led Freuhauf to an eminence it never achieved even in its old heyday. When I commented on his immaculate desk top, this taciturn Texan, with a grin and a wink, said he kept the things he needed and the things that needed his attention stashed away in convenient places behind him as well as *in* the desk. He stoutly maintained the empty surface didn't mean that his work was all done or that he had none to do.

The other mogul is Don Power, now the chairman of General Telephone & Electronics. On the two occasions I visited him at his office, he was sitting, Buddha-like, behind a large paper-bare desk, hands folded over the midriff, with a gentle, benign smile.

He looked exactly like the cat who'd swallowed the canary.

And, of course, he usually had done just that.

Under his direction GT&E swallowed up more than fifty companies from 1951 to 1966—to the immensely profitable happiness of all stockholders involved.

I was so inspired by the success of the Clean Deskers that several times I've tried like all get-out to imitate them, on the premise that this must be the secret of their success. So far the effort has been almost a total failure. I refuse to believe, however, there's a message in this. The rest of you sloppy desk types will agree, I'm sure.

12/15/67

When the corporate liquidity crunch was really on a while back, one emergency measure used by sweating cash-responsible executives was to delay paying the company's bills in their normal course.

Usually, a pretext in the form of questioning some item or other was used to cover the delay.

With the cash emergency happily and many months past, there is no longer any excuse to use this "costless" form of enforced borrowing from one's suppliers.

It's cheap stuff.

It's a crummy form of coercion-extortion.

It's high time, past time that decent companies cut it out.

3/15/72

No company can long run well and profitably without a budget. Living within it, sticking to it, is a virtue and mostly a necessity. Exceeding income estimates and performing with less expenditures than estimated is the stuff of which executive promotions are made.

But inflexibility on the Chief Executive Officer level toward budgets is the stuff of which ex-CEOs are made.

No one (except, of course, "economists" and we who forecast) can predict with decimal accuracy twelve months ahead, never mind two years and five years ahead. A sound budget is simply an intelligent estimate liberally laced with guesstimates and flavored by the pessimism or optimism that may have prevailed at the time of finalizing.

The top man is top man because he has the confidence to make a budget flexible, a guide for growth rather than a stunting strait jacket.

1/15/71

That personable dynamo who heads International Utilities Corp., Jack Seabrook, recently sat down with a group of *Forbes'* editors and made one observation, among many pertinent ones: "We like company officers who have expensive wives. They make good excutives because they're under the gun at home to make a lot of money."

Now, while there may be something in that interesting management approach, I'm sure neither you nor I would want to plant this thought at home.

9/1/72

Recently some of us here asked the chieftain of a major insurance company about the costly and too lengthy process of settling claims. In pointing out his company's success in reducing these, he attributed a major part of the improvement in both areas to the fact that his company had started using women to make offers of settlements on behalf of the insurance company.

"It's remarkable how many more people will accept a

reasonable offer of settlement from an insurance company when it's made by a woman instead of a man.

"We may not be very enthusiastic about Women's Lib, but in our company we're all in favor of Women's Lip."

11/15/72

A letter containing this tale landed on my desk:

Some of the world's greatest financiers met in Chicago in 1923—

Chairman of the largest independent steel company

Boss of the largest gas company

Greatest wheat speculator

A member of the President's cabinet

Greatest bear on Wall Street

Head of the world's greatest monopoly

They were considered among the world's most successful men. At least they had found the secret of making money. Now . . . some forty years later, where are these men?

1. Chairman of the largest independent steel company, Charles Schwab, died in debt.

2. Boss of the largest gas company, Howard Hopson, served five years in prison for defrauding his stockholders, later died in a sanitarium.

3. The greatest wheat speculator, Arthur Cutten, was facing an indictment for tax evasion at the time of his death.

4. The member of the President's cabinet, Albert Fall, went to jail for fraud.

5. The greatest bear on Wall Street, Jesse Livermore, died a suicide.

6. The head of the world's greatest monopoly, Ivar Kreuger, the match king, died a suicide.

The same year, 1923, the winner of several important
golf championships, including the PGA tournament, was
Gene Sarazen. Today he is still going strong, still playing
an excellent game of golf, and is solvent.

I can't vouch for the accuracy of all the facts in this
little tale, but in spirit it is true. All these men came to
sad and/or bad ends.

Conclusion: Stop worrying about your business. Get
out and play golf.

12/15/67

Why is it when one begins fattening with age that the young
and the doctors and the wives and the golf-crazed contemporaries unanimously, vehemently, virulently urge us-
who-do-not to exercise?

Chauncey Depew, the after-dinner raconteur, said many
things that people have kept on saying since. One I find most
apropos as response to exercisers so exercised with those of
us who have more sense—"I get my exercise being pallbearer
at the funerals of my friends who exercise."

Amen.

And may the rest of you let those of us who are fat and
lazy and alive rest in peace.

1/15/71

The ability of some men to be on the go for apparently endless hours for endless days amazes their friends and exhausts
their associates. Two types are notable for maintaining these
twenty-hour days: politicos, particularly in the weeks preced-
ing elections, and top corporate executives who, in addition
to running far-flung enterprises, shoulder without audible
groans civic responsibilities—charity-fund drives, cultural
responsibilities, school-board activities, and so forth.

"If you want to get something done, get a busy man to do it," runs the old cliché.

How do these fellows manage it?

How can they work twice as long or at least seem to get by with half the sleep the rest of us require?

They've learned the art of catnapping—snatching the proverbial forty winks in the car or cab or plane from here to there or a ten-minute snooze between appointments.

Necessity has, in the case of political campaigners, sometimes taught a man to make the most of even a few minutes, particularly for shut-eye. Soldiers, too, learn the art, with exhaustion the persuasive teacher.

A doer all the long day and most of the night was Winston Churchill, who thus in a lifetime could ring up the most prodigious accomplishments in a multitude of fields.

I don't know if this knack of snatching sleep can be taught, but if so, the professor or the school should be an enormous success. Imagine the number of energetic, ambitious men who would be delighted to keep going if they knew how to fight off the need for seven or eight hours sleep every night. Of course, they'd also have to get secretaries and associates willing and able to learn the technique.

Personally, I haven't the slightest interest in learning how to work longer and longer every day.

Climbing into the sack at night with nothing ahead but seven hours of sleep is to me one of life's unadulterated delights.

11/1/65

Usually, when a top executive sells substantial shares of his company's stock, people assume that he thinks the price is headed down.

Sometimes, that is doubtless the case.

But sometimes, you know, even a big wheel in a big company can sell his stock for the same reasons that you and I sometimes do—because he needs the money.

A man can be rich in terms of the value of the shares he holds in the company he heads, but to buy a house or golf clubs or cars or children's education takes Greenies, and occasionally stock must be sold to get 'em.

Paying taxes, too, must be done in the coin of the realm, not in the certificates of one's company. There's no need, in other words, for all of us to assume always that the poor guy who runs a company and sells some of his company's stock is bailing out because he knows something that we don't know.

He could be selling for the very reason that he's a poor guy.

Relatively speaking, of course.

11/15/67

One can't have an alphabet without letters.

Now it's getting to be that one can't have a corporation without changing its name to initials.

Which is all well and good when your corporation is that big and spends multiple millions identifying those initials. There are few who don't know what GM stands for, or GE, TWA, NCR, and A & P.

But what's with PPG? We all know Pittsburgh Plate Glass.

Contractions also seem to be in vogue. Because most people recognize Alcoa and Avco and Coke and Pan Am and Sohio, it doesn't follow that Asarco will immediately bring to mind American Smelting & Refining Company. And how about Canco? Does everyone recognize that as American Can Company?

It makes sense for Boeing Airplane to become Boeing Company. It's the word *Boeing* that has meaning. So, too, for Texas Company to be Texaco, Monsanto Chemical to become Monsanto, Singer Manufacturing Company to be Singer Company.

But somebody ought to suggest to some of these name changers that there is great value in a long-established proper name and often less than none in some collection of initials meaningless in the marketplace.

Borg-Warner means something. It's a name with meaning in its industry, to its customers, to investors.

As a corporate symbol, B-W doesn't mean a thing.

B-W's management has been smart enough to recognize an error. They decided to use their good name—Borg-Warner.

7/1/65

The editor of the magazine's "Thoughts" page passed on to me this memorandum: "I thought perhaps you might be interested in this for your editorial page." The Thought:

> As nearly everyone knows, an executive has practically nothing to do, except to decide what is to be done; to tell somebody to do it; to listen to reasons why it should not be done, why it should be done by someone else, or why it should be done in a different way; to follow up to see if the thing has been done; to discover that it has been done incorrectly; to point out how it should have been done; to conclude that as long as it has been done, it may as well be left where it is; to wonder if it is not time to get rid of a person who cannot do a thing right; to reflect that he probably has a wife and a large family, and that certainly any successor would be just as bad, and maybe worse; to consider how much simpler and better the thing would have

been done if one had done it oneself in the first place; to reflect sadly that one could have done it in twenty minutes, and as things turned out, one has to spend two days to find out why it has taken three weeks for someone else to do it wrong.

—Attributed to John L. McCaffrey,
some time ago CEO of International Harvester
11/1/70

People are talking about the new "civilized" way to fire executives.

You kick 'em upstairs.

They're given a title, a liberal tithe, nothing to do, and a secretary to do it with.

What a way to go!

10/1/66

"It's human nature."

Whatever that is, it's the favorite way of explaining the inexplicable, the rationale for the irrational. It's the only way I can think of to account for the almost invariably sour view that predecessors take toward their successors.

The more successful the successor, the greater the irk, the warmer the ire. It's even more aggravating when the predecessor himself has picked the successor.

Politics, of course, abound with colorful examples. Teddy Roosevelt was so dismayed with his handiwork, Taft, that he tried to bulldoze him into oblivion with Bull Moosers.

Unhappy Al Smith, happy-warrioring against successor Franklin Roosevelt for the Democratic presidential nomination in 1932. Most recently, Israeli father Ben-Gurion railing bitterly against chosen successor Eshkol.

Because public figures are public figures, their sour

grapes get squeezed publicly, but my bashful ears have burned more than once listening to age-retired corporate shoguns commenting on the performances and personalities of the chaps who took their seats.

Phew!

Come to think of it, however, can you imagine some young squirt doing *your* job anything like as well as you do? Worse yet, how'll we feel when the time comes that someone *does* have our job and *is* doing it better?!!

12/1/65

Prophecies Fulfilled ...

We are hell-bent to put a man on the moon. Thousands of our scarce, best scientific brains are working at it full tilt. Estimated cost of the journey: $30 billion.

Thirty billion dollars!

Is this trip necessary?

Says Warren Weaver, former president of the American Association for the Advancement of Science: "I believe that most scientists consider the proposed expenditure quite un-justified on the grounds of scientific consideration, and also consider the frantic pace of the program to be wasteful." There seems to be wide agreement that we can determine if the moon is made of green cheese by unmanned flights at a small portion of the cost of manned flights—a paltry $10 billion or so.

The only visible justification for this incredible outlay and the inevitable vast waste involved in doing it with crash programming is national prestige.

Would it be heresy to suggest that maybe this is a bit of prestige we can't afford? And don't need? Currently, Russia is one up in the space prestige race by putting two sputniks up at once. Sure, we will need to catch up in the manned space program, but for valid military and scientific reasons. An extra $15 billion or $20 billion to have a G.I. weekend on the moon, according to experts, is justified by neither of the above considerations.

In fact, I think we're ahead of the game from either angle if we let Russia keep working at it during the next decade while they raise food prices for their people by 30 percent and do away with the building of individual homes to finance it.

Why should we wander down this primrose path, or rather, why should we go broke shooting the moon path?

Prestige? Thirty billion dollars' worth?

9/1/62

Are you not surprised and pleased and proud of our country's reaction to the incredible feat of landing men on the moon?

Instead of beating our chests and chanting "On to Mars," people and Congress have reacted with a mixture of great joy and sensible cool.

With near unanimity American voices have made the point that if we can so soar in space, it's high time we brought the same sort of concentration of brains and pelf to our dire problems here on earth—pollution, poverty, transportation, education, health, inflation, etc.

Sure, say most polled citizens, keep on with the space program—but if we can learn virtually as much by unmanned space shots around and to Mars and other planets years away at a fraction of the cost of manned ones, why do the latter?

Truly, I think it is a wonderful thing that our moon achievement hasn't made us simply starry-eyed, but has served to renew our determination to deal more effectively with some pretty earthy, very present problems.

9/1/69

Sargent Shriver, Director of the Peace Corps, has asked Congress to double the size of the Corps—and, of course, double its budget.

I am sorry. I think it is a mistake.

As a supporter of the concept when it was announced and as an applauder of its great success, I think harm will result from the request itself and, if granted, there are additional dangers.

Surely, Mr. Shriver must be aware that one of the main obstacles to the creation of a separate national service corps is the fear on the part of many in Congress and the country that such an additional new federal agency will continue to proliferate far beyond the projected numbers—all according to Parkinson's law. Seeking to increase the Peace Corps from its present 6,869 workers to 13,000 next year at this time certainly lends credence to that fear.

Will doubling the size of the outfit double its effectiveness, double its success? I doubt it.

One very important ingredient of the Peace Corps' success has been its manageability *because* of its modest size. Mr. Shriver and a handful of apparently capable aides could actually see, as well as oversee, both projects and personnel. They have been able carefully to select the most capable and keenly motivated from the many applicants. They have been able for the most part to undertake the most practical and meaningful projects.

Doubling numbers and multiplying undertakings couldn't help but affect adversely the batting average.

The Peace Corps' meaning, impact, and purpose will not be proportionately furthered or strengthened by upping its numbers. Primarily, its meaning, impact, and purpose are symbolic in the broadest and best sense of the term. A handful of dedicated, qualified young Americans, at work on assorted projects in many lands, will not and were not intended to solve or resolve the problems of mankind in underdeveloped countries. They were intended to reflect, and have succeeded in reflecting, the true American image abroad better than many of our billions spent in some forms of foreign aid.

Doubling this hardy handful will have relatively little effect on the Peace Corps' broadest purpose. It does double the chance of boo-boos, pratfalls, and backfires.

The request has hurt prospects for creation of a national service corps.

The granting of it would hurt the Peace Corps itself.

7/15/63

The other day in the course of a conversation somebody asked, "Whatever happened to the Peace Corps?"

Good question.

This has been perhaps one of the most inspiring, sensible, and uncostly efforts this country has ever made in foreign affairs on a down-to-earth basis. It tapped that invaluable reservoir of goodwill, the idealism that so often motivates the decent young.

Those who volunteered and made the grade may have done far less immediate good on their assorted scenes than they hoped, but what they saw and what they did and what they learned and the frustrations they encountered resulted in citizens far more valuable to themselves and their country.

In relation to the innumerable stories one read and heard about the Peace Corps as recently as a year ago, one hears little or nothing today.

I hope it doesn't mean that there are fewer projects, fewer people involved, and lessening of government enthusiasm and support.

7/1/67

From "Fact and Comment," *Forbes*, August 1, 1963: "If instead of spending 20 million scarce dollars for three jet-propelled harems, President Achmed Sukarno devoted money to the development of facilities for tourism in his incredibly varied and beautiful Indonesia, his people and country could prosper mightily and with self-respect. After all, despite Sukarno's hostility and the viciousness of the recent volcanic eruptions, Bali still inspires the poets, and hundreds of thousands around the world would love to be able to take a look-see for themselves."

From *Life* magazine, February 1, 1969: ". . . now a luxury hotel stands waiting on its beaches, and this summer a big new jet landing strip will be completed, making Bali the most entrancing waystop on a traveler's map."

5/1/69

. . . Another—and far bigger—step toward United Europe looms immediately ahead. Six independent nations of Western Europe—West Germany, France, Belgium, Luxembourg, the Netherlands, and Italy—have already inked the treaty setting up the European Economic Community.

. . . The consequences to the United States, moreover, are hardly less dramatic than those for Europe. We cannot help but applaud the strengthening of Europe's economic and military potential as well as the weakening of the centrifugal tendencies that have always left the free nations of the West at the mercy of any determined invader.

But there is another consequence of the Common Market that we cannot ignore, either. That is the fact that it will affect our economic interests in several ways. It will probably almost certainly make Western European firms more potent competitors in the world market. Secondly, while it is making European business stronger in mass markets and mass production, it will erect and maintain a tariff barrier against American goods in markets where community members will have duty-free access. In selling goods to Italy, for example, we must look forward to the day when we will have to climb in over tariff walls while French and German competitors stroll in tariff-free.

We cannot, of course, oppose the economic community on these grounds. Nor could we stop it, even if we wanted to. Instead, it behooves farsighted American businessmen to start taking steps now to meet the situation.

8/15/58

Don't be misled by the nostalgia and the hopes and the fears and the sour grapes and the lofty platitudes which in January greeted the entry of Britain and Ireland and Denmark into the Common Market of France, Germany, Italy, Belgium, Holland, and Luxembourg. It's mostly unfortunate, but this European union has probably less unity in fact and certainly less unity in spirit than existed for several years after World

War II. Then, fear of Russia, floods of dollars, and total
weariness of hate, bombs, blood, and death unified the free
countries of Europe as never before. Their voices often or-
chestrated under the baton of the Star-Spangled Man with
Whiskers.

Today's vaunted formalized unity is nothing more than
a tariff-protected trade area. Despite being a bit leaky and
somewhat wobbly, the Common Market, though, is a fact
that is affecting our own trade balance as well as those of
Japan and the world's unmembered countries.

A power center, however, either militarily or politically,
Europe isn't, and there is little prospect of its soon, if ever,
being such. The Common Market nine remain with little in
common except those things that divide them—each's na-
tionalism, culture, language and traditional ire of one for
other.

To think of Europe as a fact is fiction. Be it ever so
regrettable, for Europe the whole still remains far less than
its parts.

2/15/73

... This writer obtained the impression of France as a country that has lost faith in itself. There is no confidence that,
through boldness and leadership, they can rebuild their economy. There is no confidence that, through statesmanship, they
can play a leading part in formulating new and wider policies
vital for the survival of free nations.

One can easily understand, after the bitter blood-wringer
that this nation has gone through since World War I, why
this psychology of pessimism and defeat is so prevalent. It
is not hard to understand why the average Frenchman wants
to hang on to today's bits of sunshine, and to resist coming to
grips with the tough realities of tomorrow. He has had his
bitter cupful of yesterday's realities, and refuses to believe

that tomorrow's possibilities, even if they happen, could be any worse than what he has been through.

Probably, France's greatest single need at the moment is a French Churchill, who could inspiringly sum up their problem and rally them all to tackle it, based on their own rich tradition of valor and grandeur.

11/1/54

In the declining days of 1958, President Charles de Gaulle broadcast to the people of France his proposals for higher taxes and curtailed spending. His words were hauntingly reminiscent of the "blood, sweat, and tears" theme with which de Gaulle's old ally and adversary Winston Churchill once rallied the British people. Needless to say, de Gaulle's proposals for blood, sweat, and higher taxes brought forth some grumbling. But grumbling is only human. The truly impressive thing was the way the French people seemed ready to accept a measure of discipline from de Gaulle that they had refused from a number of his well-meaning but powerless predecessors.

1/15/59

NATO as a credible force-in-being is as good as dead.

The hand that held the dagger was de Gaulle's, but this assassin's success, ironically enough, was only possible because of NATO's own success in fulfilling it mission.

The tears at the bier need not be bitter.

NATO came into the world when Western Europe faced the imminent possibility of being overrun by Stalin's Red Army. I share the belief of most responsible West European statesmen that this danger is past.

Knowing full well that the American atomic shield will continue to shelter free Europe, and knowing that Russia isn't about to invade NATO lands, de Gaulle has really relished uprooting the alliance. More than three years ago on this page (*Forbes*, March 1, 1963) I wrote: "As de Gaulle flexes his newfound muscles, he is certainly going to move as quickly as he dares to splinter NATO. He regards it simply as an American scheme that stands athwart his own vague Grand Design for a de Gaulle Europe. If de Gaulle lives long enough, NATO, as it now exists, will be dead."

He did, and it is.

6/15/66

Lockheed is just too large a company to go on with what appears to be complacent satisfaction with its position and image.

Because neither is what it used to be.

I'm not talking about bucks and backlog, but of something of far greater long-run consequences to its customers and stockholders: what the name Lockheed conjures, connotes in the minds and hearts of its countrymen.

This giant may not be selling notions over the counter in the country-store sense of notions, but what you and I and a few million other Americans think of Lockheed *is* important to the handful of customers who order what Lockheed sells. For some time it has been apparent this company's prime concern has been only with Pentagonians. Even airline presidents haven't been courted since the Electra met with its mixed results. . . .

Lockheedians, you have had a great past. For a future on that par, look up, look out.

2/1/67

When Eugene McCarthy voted against Teddy Kennedy and for Louisiana's Senator Long for Democratic whip, it seemed to open one eye of some of his fervent followers.

When he begged off the Foreign Relations Committee with the practical result of giving his seat to a howling hawk, it opened the other eye of the same some.

Forbes told 'em so way back when the young were going ape on his behalf, under the illusion he was for and against what they were for and against.

Months ago, when I suggested here that he had a sour soul soothed only by an outsized ego, the bedraggled and bedazzled followers of the pied poet were outraged.

The dimensions of the man haven't changed.

Their smallness only lately became more apparent to more people.

2/1/69

PROGRESS THAT ISN'T

SST.

12/15/70

Invest private capital in South America today? Not unless you consider wagering at roulette or at a crap game an investment. You might even—eventually—break even, but to consider putting money in Latin America as an investment in the ordinary sense of the word is foolish. It is a gamble.

3/15/63

World wars are now passé. Peace as it now exists is here to stay. Why? Because world peace no longer depends on having a climate of moral "good" prevail, nor does it depend on a concert of great powers agreeing not to disagree while they jointly whack up the spoils as in pre–World War I days. Nor does it depend on the fragile unanimity or facsimile thereof in a League of Nations or a United Nations. The scientists have wrought the miracle, where men of goodwill, where the Machiavellis and the Pax Romana boys have all failed.

The atom bomb quite promptly ended the last war; its offspring, the hydrogen bomb, makes a future world conflict by those who possess it utterly fruitless, utterly pointless.

So long as the United States keeps its "military posture"—that is, the capacity to retaliate by being able to lob back to the country of origin hydrogen bomb for hydrogen bomb—the safety of our own country and the free world is assured against the old-fashioned assault of thundering tanks and marching men. The United States should now concentrate abroad on winning the cold war with new weapons, not military ones. We should not insist on making the new nations of the world over in our image; we should understand that the economic facts of life as yet make the democracy we know impossible for these new nations. They need sympathetic understanding; they deserve our patience; we should extend our help when asked, not in the form of a Washington-conceived blueprint for their betterment, but in the ways that their leaders, and they, feel will most help them. If these countries don't want what we think they should have, let's not force it on them.

To ensure the peace, we need only maintain our capacity to retaliate.

We can concentrate more than ever before on the war of ideas and ideals, where we have often bumbled and fumbled. We are learning the hard way that it is not good enough simply to want to do good.

In a sense we are at the sort of millennium that should be meat and potatoes for a nation that has no interest in militarism and conquest. We are in a position of world leadership—the first time in history—when hot wars embracing the globe are out the window. We are in a position of world leadership when ideas and understanding can be tested throughout the world.

But it is a far tougher struggle than most people had imagined.

5/1/56

According to word now seeping from Authoritative Sources in the Pentagon, the United States is planning to put yet *another* 300,000 American soldiers in South Vietnam, bringing our total there to 600,000.

Now that the military is geared up for the training of additional tens of thousands, now that these additional thousands are beginning to emerge from the pipeline, draft quotas climb steadily, steeply.

If 300,000 cannot do whatever it is we are ultimately planning to do, neither will 600,000. If we hold steadily to the present "course," whatever it is, in Southeast Asia, by a year from now we will probably need another doubling.

Rumblings out of Thailand indicate it may soon need more American "advisers," more American "security" for the 28,000 Americans now manning our Thai bases, more Americans to handle the increased pipelines—more, more, more American manpower on the Asian mainland.

How bloody dumb can we get?

It's incredible, but apparently true, that there are people in the Pentagon who believe we can secure the future of the United States by putting increasing hundreds of thousands of armed American youngsters on the Asian continent.

Can't anyone in the Administration see the absurdity of our pleas to Russia to help turn off the Vietnam conflict? Why for one moment would she seriously try to do so when we are committing more and more of our resources and people to doing *her* battle with Red China?

Before it is forever too late can we not *stop* escalating? Why, why, why can't we stand and hold?

Russia and China, with their 4,500-mile common border, age-old quarrels, and century-old enmities, with their polemic bitterness at new intensity, should be left to confront each other. The spectacle of the United States being the Russian bear's-paw on the Asiatic mainland defies sensible comprehension.

I have no patience, no truck with the vociferous, foolhardy few who say we should get out of South Vietnam lock, stock, and barrel in present circumstances.

But damn it, it's high time to cease the doubling of our own manpower stakes in Asia every few months.

9/15/66

The Watergate affair is producing the biggest White House exodus since the British burned the place down in 1814. People have likened it to the Teapot Dome scandal. The analogy's inaccurate and inadequate. In Teapot Dome a Cabinet level money payoff was the shocker.

At Watergate it was the Constitution and the rights of a free people that got ripped off. One could feel less alarm, less aghast if a greed for money had motivated the plotters. Bribery and corruption in high places have long been known to man.

It's the blindness to what the Presidency really is, what democracy and the Constitution are all about that's most scary. That those trusted by the man who has the greatest responsibility for preserving all those things could be involved in a Watergate is incomprehensible.

5/15/73

From Watergate, little positive will come. Sure, it'll be a while anyway before a President's top staffers again act as if that affinity puts them above the law, entitles them to trample on the constitutional rights of less exalted citizens guilty or suspected of unRight thinking, unRight acting.

But the great good, the most essential change that could emerge from Watergate would be tough and near-total changes in political-campaign financing.

Really Big Money Givers naturally have a reason, a motive. It could even conceivably (by whom I don't know) be a good one. But Big Money campaign giving, be it by a corporation or union or individual or association, should be forbidden with enforceable effectiveness. A ceiling of, say, a thousand bucks, in any one election or any one year. Candidates *and* parties should be limited to fixed amounts or percentages that they can spend, with the winner's election voided if it's exceeded.

For national, and perhaps state, elections, TV and radio time should be free and strictly apportioned (and in mercifully limited amounts).

People can remain free to give of themselves and their time just as much as they want for a candidate or a party or both.

It's the towering cost and raising it that's been the source of most of what's bad in our present campaign system.

In this case, the cancer is identifiable and removable.

I'll give you big odds, though, it won't happen.

Maddening, isn't it?

11/1/73

... And Prophecies Unfulfilled

PROFUNDITY

It's better to be wrong sometimes than all the time.

9/1/71

FORECASTING

Crystal-balling is a hazardous occupation. Those of us who sometimes do it are saved, when we drop the ball, by the fortunately short memories of our busy, doing readers.

1/1/67

Before prognosticating this New Year, I thought you might relish reading the devastating, near-total forecast wrongs I wrote here exactly a year ago:

FORECAST 1973:

EVERYTHING GOOD <u>COULD</u> HAPPEN

It's hard to believe, harder even to contemplate, what a good, almost *all*-good economic year 1973 will be. Anywhere and everywhere you turn, the odds heavily favor very favorable progress:

• No wars, and the present one done with.

• Quite likely, the miracle of a signed, quite real détente-peace between Israel and Egypt, Jordan, and Lebanon.

• Significant, solid growth of our real GNP *unac*companied by runaway inflation. This I believe, because President Nixon will persuade even the stupidest Greedy of Business and Labor to act with relative restraint as controls come off in bits and pieces and, finally, *in toto*.

• Again, under discerning and determined presidential direction, the fully resolvable confrontation among ecologists, energists, and business expansionists will happen. They'll recognize the necessity and sense of working together, though they may take a bit longer to learn to love one another.

• Even the dollar faces a happy 1973. With our inflation relatively slower than that of most lands with whom we trade, our unaffordable trade imbalance will move substantially toward greater balance. Foreign money will flow at a rate into the United States for investments and things, and haven.

• Thus, when we sit down, as sit down we must and will, to progress toward a new monetary system, the voice of America will no longer be weak and unrespected but stronger and more nearly equal.

• Unemployment will be significantly less by year's end.

• With wars done, the draft done, and more jobs available, almost all young Americans will complete the shift from unnatural despair to their more natural state of hope and confidence that their country and the world may become better for millions more.

• This unblemished economic outlook and the dollar's prospective new muscle, of course, are strongly buttressed by the President's announced, pronounced determination to whack with will and results at the federal deficit. While he can do only part of it by executive order, he'll go to the people if necessary to slow down Congress' irresponsible Spenders Unlimited.

• Further underpinning, further impetus to this Good Year is the other "impossible"—no new or additional federal taxes this year or even the next. Who says so? The President. As more and more people are coming to learn, they'd better learn to believe him and what he says. In recent years, less and less has he said things out of political necessity instead of personal conviction.

What a forecast, what an unblemished outlook for 1973! Almost scary, isn't it?

To quote selectively from the above—"What a forecast. ... Almost scary, isn't it?"

If you look carefully, perhaps you can find a stray line or two that wasn't utterly wide of the mark. Rather than having hit any nails on the head, it would appear I must have holes in my own.

So-o-o, since my forcasting accuracy now has absolutely

nowhere to go but up, you can be sure that at least a fraction of this forecast will be Right On:

1974 won't be *all* bad.

In answer, then, to the question of What Lies Ahead, I can truthfully say: the ones I write here.

1/1/74

With it reasonably certain who will be inaugurated President a few days from now, speculative interest has turned to the question of who's next. Since *Forbes'* readers are accustomed, when not deciding matters themselves, to finding out what's going on now and what is likely to be happening in the foreseeable future, we thought they'd like to know the answer. (For some people, four years down the road might not be considered foreseeable, but not for Fearless Forbes.)

In 1976 the Republican nomination will go (on the first ballot, yet) to Spiro Agnew—despite spirited attempts by Illinois Senator Charles Percy to convince, in primaries and smoke-filled rooms, the Republican nomination determiners that it will take a more liberal nominee to have a chance against the Democratic candidate . . .

. . . who will be (on the first ballot and by acclamation) Senator Edward Kennedy.

The winner and the next President of the United States?

Ted Kennedy—and by a considerably wider margin than his brother Jack's when he nosed out Richard Nixon in 1960.

Before you start writing me angry letters about why this script *shouldn't* happen, please remember it's not a statement of what *should* happen but of what *will* happen.

1/1/73

Harry Truman's nomination by the Democratic Convention has been greeted with glee and a high degree of relief by all hoping for a Republican Administration after the fall election. According to every current poll, the strong Dewey-Warren ticket will swamp the Truman-Barkley slate.

The whole bizarre, pathetic Administration of Mr. Truman demonstrates again the clear, sharp fact that while indeed anyone in this democracy *can* be President, only men of extraordinary ability, experience, and perception can be *good* Presidents, *effective* leaders.

Most people grant Mr. Truman's good intentions, and feel embarrassed at the sight of his painfully inadequate attempts to steer this country with more success than his haberdashery. His efforts to turn the political tide by the demagogic call for a special session of Congress have already begun to backfire. This bit of super-smart politics indeed provides the impoverished Democratic National Committee with a free forum and free radio time, but it is doubtful if this sample of administrative political trickery will suggest to the American voter that the Truman advisers are especially well fitted to provide the nation with four more years of "leadership."

Dewey, able campaigner and no loafer, will wage an aggressive fight all the way. By not taking for granted the victory most predict, he will make it doubly sure.

And in January the country will begin to experience, after sixteen years, a leadership that has confidence in the ability of Americans to govern themselves.

8/1/48

Talk wells and swells about the prospect of wage-price controls à la World War II unless inflation very soon abates. Even I waved this shirt while urging extension of the surtax and other inflation-abating measures.

Now that so many are talking about it, it's about time to point out that the imposition of such total federal controls by President Nixon and/or the Congress is about as likely to happen as, say, the repeal of the income tax or the dissolution of unions.

7/15/69

Any day now Richard Nixon is supposed to announce whether he will be a candidate for governor of California next year. As one of a steadily dwindling number who has not yet been asked for advice, I am glad to give it.

If there is anything deader in politics than yesterday's unsuccessful candidate, it's the same fellow planning to try again without a firm, elected political basis. The exceptions, as usual, merely prove the rule.

If Richard Nixon desires to be the Republican presidential nominee again either in 1964 or (with more perspicacity) in 1968, he should take the advice of one whose political career doesn't qualify him to give it—Dick, if you don't become governor of California, you're dead.

9/15/61

I've heard, read, and, I guess, even written some drivel in my lifetime, but nothing to equal the pundits' "serious" speculations about whether or not President Johnson will run again in 1968.

The day that there's no next day will be the day that L.B.J. retires as a presidential possibility.

It's all well and good and, actually, quite expected of Republican politicians to speechify solemnly about such tripe, but tripe is an essential stock-in-trade for a politician.

Not for pundits taken seriously by their readers.

You can begin with the total certainty that President Johnson will run again, and with every drop in his Gallup, you can bet your Texas boots that this total certainty becomes totally certainer.

The un-asylumed man who envisions L.B.J. declining

the 1968 Democratic presidential nomination because of hurt feelings and a low poll pulse, and graciously handing the prize to Bobby, must be a disciple of Dr. Leary.

1/1/67

Those people who always know everything have been telling us for a long time how dead certain it is that President Johnson won't be reelected.

Wanna bet?

It's one thing to be fed up with, sore at the White House incumbent, but something totally different to translate that into a ballot for somebody else.

While L.B.J. may be caught with his polls down now, ten months from today, vis-à-vis a specific alternative candidate, it could be a very different story.

A sitting President, even a dumb one, is never to be confused with a sitting duck.

Lyndon Johnson isn't dumb.

He isn't going to be sitting.

And he ain't no duck.

The dumb ones are those who think that he is dead politically.

1/15/68

With surprising frequency in politics as in other matters, things have quite the opposite effect from what has been predicted and intended. Both before and at the time that Senator Eugene McCarthy announced his candidacy for the Democratic nomination, most everyone saw this as a serious complication for L.B.J.

With the President's poll popularity relatively nil, it was assumed Senator McCarthy would do very well in the primaries he entered. All the unhappy and all the disgruntled—

who then seemed like most of the Democrats—would have a place to polarize. The ever growing doubts about the wisdom of our course in Vietnam could be expressed, and so forth.

As a matter of fact, McCarthy's candidacy will have almost the opposite effects.

McCarthy has no Kefauver image, and I think in most of the primaries in which he opposes Johnson or a Johnson slate, he will do so badly that the President will look stronger in popular esteem than he actually is.

Those many who question the wisdom of the President's course of acceleration in Vietnam certainly don't want primary contests between the President and Mr. McCarthy to be considered a referendum on the war's course.

The fact of the matter is that Senator McCarthy's candidacy is turning out to be one of the better political things that has happened to President Johnson recently.

1/15/68

At this time when everybody is deploring or applauding the plethora of Democratic presidential aspirants, I predict all—or nearly all—the perspiring aspiring will have expired by convention time, that there will be a first-ballot nominee in Miami.

Having a spotty (to use the most charitable word) record in the field of political predicting, I am fearlessly prepared to be wrong again.

But just run down the list of hopefuls and a bit of elementary analysis reduces the many to one probability, with the rest unlikely to be hit by convention lightning.

Jackson? Favorite of the hard hats, his principal distinction is in being the only hopeful who is an outspoken Vietnam hawk. 'Nuff said.

Bayh? A new face, indeed, but from it comes an inex-

haustible supply of exhausted clichés. Combining this talent
with a facile cleverness at avoiding answers and positions
leaves him flat on his new face.

McCarthy? Nineteen sixty-eight's different drummer
has turned out to be as hollow as some of us said. No real
number of young will march to that empty beat again.

Kennedy? There are many indications that, fairly or
unfairly, an increasing majority of voters clearly don't feel he
is the stuff of which they prefer to have Presidents made.

Mills? This astute, tough Congressional power center is
the likeliest dark horse should deadlock move the action from
klieg-lit convention floor to smoke-filled back rooms.

Humphrey? This warm, infinitely informed and complete gentleman has all the heart and head it takes to be a
great President. But for all the wrong reasons, he remains
a victim to the Johnson Administration's mistakes.

Lindsay? His defection will win no discernible affection
in Democratic roll calls.

McGovern? If he could talk face to face with enough
young and many of their parents, he'd stand a good chance.
In the unlikely event that he could win a couple of early
primaries, McGovern would be the only plausible threat to
the far-out-front front runner, who is

Muskie.

He has to beat himself, and isn't apt to.

9/1/71

When my children want to suggest politely that a fellow is
nuts, they sometimes say, "He's buggy." I don't know what
the German slang is, but it's my guess that many a Volkswagen shareholder will soon be applying that phrase to the
management.

They have just started messing around with the most

successful four-wheeled phenomenon since the covered wagon —the Volkswagen.

Better known as the Beetle or the Bug.

Now they've come out with a VW Fastback, a nondescript-looking imitation of 100 other cars.

Not content with this bit of heresy, they've even come out with a Squareback, an equally nondescript-looking vehicle that is a four-wheeled insult to the famous man-sized VW "box" wagon.

Just because Rolls-Royce has brought out an unlikely new model, is that any reason for the Bug people to get totally out of line with a whole new line?

You know, I am rapidly coming to the conclusion that the hardest thing for doers to learn to do is to let a good thing alone.

12/11/65

VOLKSWAGEN

At the present, anyway, its future is behind it.

People get tired even of good things, and after so many years, people are simply tired of the Beetle. Many are turning to money's-worth Japanese alternatives.

Maybe at this bedtime someone should tell VW the Tale of Henry I and his too-long affair with the "T."

3/15/72

Vast millions of dollars more are going to be needed from investors before pay TV becomes a coupon clipper's reality. It's coming, though.

Progress has been slow and costly, and the problems and complications have been far greater than we rosy optimists of many years ago foresaw.

Twelve years ago on these pages I expressed great enthusiasm about pay TV: "The possibilities . . . are limitless."

Eight years ago I concluded another editorial supporting pay TV with these words: "Probably all manner of conflicting 'vested interests' have selfish economic reasons for throwing roadblocks in the path of a sensibly regulated pay-as-you-see television system, but there is a sufficient pot of gold at the end of the rainbow to keep its advocates plugging. And as the public increasingly realizes the value of subscription television, they will translate their desires into a demand that will break through the barriers of opposition and FCC red tape. The sooner the better."

Those words are as valid today as they were then, only the payoff on pay TV will not be delayed another twelve years—perhaps another three or four.

6/1/64

Recession?

Forget it. It's not in the cards.

Here and there a bit of bloom will be off the boom— and a good thing too.

But recession?

No.

Far, far from it.

9/1/68

Is an economic slowdown coming?

Pssst! It's here.

11/1/69

Sell Investment Advice— Don't Follow It

Rarely here do we ever give specific stock market suggestions. We make more money selling advice than following it. But with major airline stocks still much more down than they once were up, you can safely take a profitable flyer on the best-managed biggies such as American, Delta, and United.

7/15/72

Here, some months ago (July 15, 1972) I wrote that I thought airline stocks were a good buy.

In the interval they've had assorted ups (which only a chartist could find) and pretty continuous downs. I still think I'm right, and am most happy to note that the fabulous dean of *Forbes'* columnists, Lucien Hooper, commented in the February 15 issue: "If I were to pick out one group that I think is selling at what will prove to be below central value this year, it would be the airlines."

With three notable exceptions, the airlines these days are being well managed, and they are—most of 'em—essential.

They'll go up.

3/15/73

Some *Forbes* subscribers have written asking me why, after enthusing about airline stocks when they were selling much higher than today, I'm quiet on the subject these days.

Don't you think there's plenty to be quiet about?

But. . . .

One of these days (may you all live so long), I'll be able to say "I told you so."

6/15/73

I doubt if anyone in Wall Street had ever heard of New Hampshire's Democratic Senator, Thomas J. McIntyre, until August 15 this year. Now, I don't think that Wall Street will ever hear the end of Thomas J. McIntyre.

In the course of the Capitol Hill hearings on the proposed SEC additional regulations of mutual funds, the Senator allowed as how he had thrown darts at the stock market tables one day and his "selections" performed better than most mutual funds.

I couldn't resist the temptation either.

The other day *Forbes'* editor Jim Michaels, publisher

Jim Dunn, and yours truly pitched darts against that day's *New York Times* stock exchange tables.

Two of the three of us substantially outperformed the mutual funds. Guess who did worse—far worse.

The results of an assumed $10,000 investment, $1,000 in each of ten stocks, was compared with the results of the most recent Forbes Mutual Fund Survey. In a recent five-year period Jim Dunn's portfolio outperformed 69 percent of all stock funds; Jim Michaels' portfolio outperformed 64 percent, while my dart hits outperformed only 46 percent. In a recent twelve-month period Dunn outperformed 76 percent; Michaels, 62 percent, and yours truly, 24 percent.

Now if any of you really think we're advocating this method of investing, you're out of your mind. After all, Forbes, Inc., makes some of its money selling stock market advice (not following it, of course).

However, if I were running Parker Brothers, the Boston game makers, I would figure out some way of marketing this game.

11/1/67

Ofttimes people ask *Forbes* for specific advice on what securities to buy, what they should do with ones they have, etc. *Forbes* magazine's advice on specifics is confined to the signed columns of its financial editors in another section. One of the best guideposts that can be applied by readers contemplating buying or selling of securities are the guideposts developed by Joseph D. Goodman, for more than twenty years one of this publication's financial editors.

Some profitable order could be brought to the investor's market approach by the application of these nine rules:

1. *Never buy a stock that won't go up in a bull market. The insiders are out of it.*

For some valid reason, the "informed" money is not buying that stock. The reason may not be apparent, but it exists nevertheless.

2. *Never sell a stock short that won't go down in a bear market. The insiders have it.*

Here, again, there is a compelling reason behind the scenes. Even when the facts are not clear, it's best not to "buck" the stock.

3. *Sell the stock short that won't go up in a bull market the moment the market turns to the bear side.*

A stock that can't attract buying support when everything else is moving ahead must have something radically wrong with it. It, therefore, would be vulnerable in a bear market.

4. *Buy the stock that won't go down in a bear market. It will probably lead the next rise.*

This is one of the best rules in Wall Street. It means that support is so strong that new buying will push it up when a bull cycle reappears.

5. *Don't buy the "sympathy" stock.*

Buying the sympathy stock is one of the greatest possible fallacies. There's no necessary reason why Southern Pacific or Northern Pacific should go up just because Union Pacific does. The common word *Pacific* has nothing to do with it.

6. *When a bull market turns to bear, sell the stock that has gone up the most, as it will react the most.*

This may seem to be a contradiction to Rule No. 3 above, but it isn't. Actually, the stocks that have had the greatest *percentage* rise frequently have a corrective *percentage* decline when the tide turns.

7. *Also sell the stock that has gone up the least. It couldn't go up and, therefore, must go down.*

This is in agreement with Rule No. 3. If the stock can't attract buyers, it frequently will attract sellers.

8. *When a bear market turns to bull, buy the stock that has gone down the most and also the stock that has gone down the least.*

These two principles are not opposed to each other. Instead, they illustrate two extremes in the market. Stocks showing the greatest *percentage* declines are normally due for *percentage* gains. Stocks that have held up best have a reason for doing so, hence, are in a position to attract new support.

9. *If a stock is a purchase or a sale, action should be taken at once. The market does not consider your trade in its fluctuations.*

In other words, *if buying or selling is imperative*, action should be taken at once. Such transactions should be made immediately at the market.

9/1/55

A month ago I outlined here "Nine Golden Rules of Wall Street," as developed by *Forbes'* longtime financial editor, Joseph D. Goodman. These have aroused considerable comment and some criticism from investors throughout the country. Wrote one, "Most people today have substantial profits on their investments. What are some of the most common errors made by investors leading to losses in the stock market?" Fourteen of the most common mistakes made by the public according to our own studies include:

1. Failure to have a well-defined investment plan

governed by your individual circumstances—age, dependents, objectives, etc.

2. Buying on tips from well-meaning friends. Such tips are often costly. Trained investors use *facts* and scientific principles instead.

3. Lack of patience to hold good stocks through weak or indecisive market periods until conditions improve.

4. Not enough courage to buy after prolonged decline when stocks are real bargains but news is bad and pessimism prevalent.

5. Purchasing primarily because current dividend yield is high. Better check fifteen- to twenty-year dividend record for consistency.

6. Investing in an industry without ascertaining whether this industry's outlook is one of growth or stagnation.

7. Being too greedy and failing to take substantial profits in time. Nobody is able to forecast *exact* top or bottom of any move.

8. Buying stocks without investigating net current asset position, earnings, inventories, and other data readily available.

9. Buying or selling stocks on basis of seasonal factors or strikes, politics, war, peace, etc.

10. Staying with a situation definitely known to be deteriorating instead of taking a loss and switching into much more promising issue to regain capital depreciation.

11. Disregard of one of the cardinal principles of investment—diversification. "Don't put all your eggs in one basket!"

12. Neglecting to keep an up-to-date record of all gains and losses so as to plan not to be unnecessarily penalized by the capital gains tax.

13. Failure to maintain adequate reserve for buying on reactions to average down initial purchase price.

14. Trying to buy at the bottom, or trying to save one-fourth or one-half of a point. Many big moves have been lost by investors putting in orders below the market, and having stock move so fast they never got aboard. It is often wise to buy at the market if you are reasonably sure of your facts and have examined market indices.

10/1/55

The overwhelmingly important factor in determining my father's personal security purchases was his opinion of the company's top management. "If the man at the wheel has character and brains, his company and my shares in it will do well."

Through almost a lifetime of knowledge of most heads of major American companies, he was in a unique position to evaluate their qualities. This was virtually his sole guide for his own investing. No earnings record, no charts, no prospects could induce him to buy stock in a company where he had a poor opinion of the boss.

Sometimes, he missed the boat. One time when a new president took over, he sold out some stock in a company whose shares later multiplied many, many times in value. "I didn't like the fellow. I thought he was arrogant and knew him to be mean, nasty, with those under him." Most times, however, his yardstick proved a reliable one.

His sky-high opinion of Cities Service's late W. Alton Jones led him to invest proportionally large amounts in that company during the late thirties. His opinion of the brains possessed by Alfred P. Sloan and the genius of Charles F. Kettering led him into General Motors stock. As he watched the immensely effective, truly teamwork concept of management of this giant in operation, he remained a stockholder all his life.

It is very difficult to evaluate management ability. There is no mathematical criterion, no Bureau of Standards scale. Yesterday's management decisions are measured in today's marketplace. Today's performance is no guarantee of tomorrow's.

As Chrysler stockholders discovered three years ago, yesterday's successes—even if they continue for some decades —are no guarantee of future successes. A few wrong decisions and this former blue chip was in most shaky shape. What brought it from its low of 9¼ in 1961 to its current 39 per share? Guidance by a not-so-dumb cluck by the name of George H. Love, who took on the critical Chrysler problems when his Consolidation Coal invested in the distressed shares. (Consolidation now owns 1.4 million shares.) In a word, new brains at the top brought this $2 billion company back from the brink.

A sensible investor indeed looks at the record, the company's present position in its industry, earnings, growth, dividend record. He considers the industry's prospects and the company's past record in research, new products, pioneering. That's all history. *History.*

In buying now, however, the investor is buying a company's *future.* Are the men heading it today the ones responsible for its recent performance? If so, how long have they guided its destinies? Many a company's fortunes have declined when the head man refused to give up control in his declining years. If there is a new chief executive officer, what's his record?

In buying stock, buy brains and you'll profit.

2/15/64

Precipitously dumping a huge block of a corporate stock is the sort of utter stupidity that one shouldn't expect (but one has come to) of big block holders.

It sometimes produces a spectacular plummet that day in the stock's price—and a headline the next day that usually produces more of the same.

It shouldn't, though.

In today's stock market the Little Guy represents what liquidity and real pulse there yet is in stock markets. He shouldn't (and fortunately is learning not to) panic at the super price changes momentarily produced by sophisticated money managers' maladroitness.

There is just no way—other than a stunning revelation of fraud or bombshell bankruptcy—that can make a share of Wrigley worth $162 at the beginning of the day and $131.75 at the end of it.

A stock most certainly will seldom stay worth exactly what you paid for it. More often than not, it gets to be worth more if it is soundly purchased in the first place. You've no real loss or profit until you sell it.

Don't be unduly alarmed at spectacular price spasms occasionally produced by Big Blockheads.

3/1/72

Most of us, when we think of investing, think in terms of buying stocks and bonds in companies making and distributing things or services.

But many a man has made and is making multiple millions in real estate.

In a few decades the 3,322 initial residents of Miami have seen their village become a city of a million residents, swelled the year round by additional hundreds of thousands of vacationers. Nor is Miami unique. Much of the rest of

Florida burgeons at a pace good trotters would envy. So, too, Arizona and California. Nor is the soaring value in real estate confined to the sunny states. Look around you in your own suburbia or city block: Anywhere, U.S.A. Consider what you paid for your country acreage or your city plot a few or many years ago. With rare exception, today it would command a far higher price.

Does all this mean that buying real estate is a sure way to multiply your money?

Personally, I'm a skeptic. It goes back to a couple of those childhood experiences that psychologists make so much money interpreting.

My mother and father were close friends of a couple who had made literally millions in the initial Florida boom of the twenties. They used to arrive at our home in Englewood, New Jersey, in a seemingly endless, chauffeured limousine and distributed to us children the most wonderful big presents. Then came the Florida bust in 1926. Within weeks they were stony broke, and Dad was lending them money to pay the rent on a small two-room New York apartment.

My other youthful memory of money in real estate goes back to the beginning of the George Washington Bridge construction. Everyone apparently was sure that at the Bridge's completion all the wooded land on the New Jersey side for miles around would be promptly inundated by the Big City cliff dwellers. Rough roads were cut through the woods, and buses would arrive from New York, while real-estate promoters under great tents would auction off numbered lots. It was all very exciting.

After a few months nothing more seemed to happen. The "roads" again grew green. The Depression arrived. And it wasn't until twenty-seven years later that what had been foretold took place. Now the whole area is a ranch-house-studded suburbia with a vengeance. But I'll wager not one in a thousand of the initial investors still held title to a square foot of the property they so eagerly bought in 1928.

Look, too, at what can happen within a city. There was a time when New York's Fourteenth Street was infinitely more valuable business property than the Fifties on Fifth Avenue. Today most of it is occupied by one- and two-story "taxpayers" and neglected loft buildings.

I guess for those who know what they're doing—and doing it themselves—real-estate investing and developing has been, is, and will continue to be quite a bonanza. But unimaginative, unknowledgeable me will string along with more mundane investments—like AT&T.

3/1/62

For as long as there has been a stock market, some people whose stocks went down instead of up have accused Wall Street of robbing them. In the last couple of years though, robbing Wall Street has reached a vogue of epidemic proportions, and the victims' naïveté has had some bizarre results.

Sometimes, staid brokers with rolltop-desk-like office procedures didn't even know for weeks and months that millions in securities were gone until someone found a few or a customer asked for some. Theft of stock certificates has reached such size that, according to an assistant district attorney covering the area, leaders of organized crime have a stock black market, where they "bargain like crazy" over prices. Someone soon, I suppose, will be able to run daily quotations on the more popular stolen stocks for the guidance of astute investors.

The whole costly debacle is just one more compelling

reason for doing away with the physical transfer of stock certificates and substituting data processing—à la our use of checks instead of cash.

8/15/71

The SEC has promulgated many useful, needed rules for the securities industry, but one of their more recent proposals must be either a late or early April fool joke. It would require that some security salesman find out all about the financial condition of a customer before making any recommendations.

On the premise that a rich guy can afford punk advice or a poor one should get only profitable advice?

Protecting investors from crooks and crooked practices is one thing. Determining *who* is allowed to buy securities is totally another.

What outlandish presumption.

That suggestion is almost on a par with this unbelievable nifty from a recent *New York Times* editorial: "The SEC would be even fairer [sic] to both the investor and the industry if it permitted fees to be related to performance. That would reward the best investment managers and penalize those with the poorest records."

!?X=¢+*#;@%&$!

And doctors, I suppose, are to be paid in proportion to the quickness of their cure, including nothing if under their care the patient expires.

And *The New York Times* will vary its advertising rates according to whether or not the advertisement and the advertiser make much, little, or no money from the space bought.

Who says the *Times* doesn't sometimes run comics?

1/15/67

Skirts are not the only things that have fashionable ups and downs. The business world, too, has fashions.

It was just a couple of economic seasons ago that a big boodle of cash in the corporate till was widely considered a sign of stupid or bad or lazy management—and sometimes a combination of all three.

You see, bags of cash attracted conglomerators as bags of cash attract plain(er) crooks. So companies, even the largest, fearing raiders, lowered their profiles by lowering the cash in the till.

And why, just a couple of economic seasons ago, was "idle" cash considered an indication of bad management or lazy management? Because it meant management didn't have this money out at work. It just sat idly collecting interest of course. But who couldn't make corporate money make more money than merely the prevailing rate of interest?

Now look.

Presto!

A new fashion!

Cash is back "in"!

Denigrating liquidity has been dropped quicker than hemlines. A management is now saluted if it *has* some cash, has some liquidity, doesn't have to go to the money market at huge interest rates to get the wherewithal to keep going and growing.

Along with Ben Franklin, my father and your father would understand and applaud this new economic fashion. I am not sure, though, they'd have ever understood why liquidity and cash went completely out of style.

6/1/70

Wouldn't you know that it would be Litton Industries that would go to the ultimate absurdity in "observing" SEC regulations against touting its stock while a new issue is pending. I don't know if it was dumbness or craftiness or thoughtfulness that prompted their CEO's decision to hold the Litton annual meeting and to tell the stockholders absolutely nothing. Not even the quarterly earnings (it eventually developed there were some).

The SEC's preclusion of a company's artificially whooping it up through advertising, press releases, officer speeches, and other drumbeating aimed at inflating demand before a new stock issue makes sense. Going to the opposite extreme and dropping a curtain on pertinent corporate information normally due at normal intervals is a cop-out that neither the SEC nor the courts should encourage or condone in any way whatsoever. The crime of concealment from investors of information equals if not exceeds that of craftily timed revealment.

Forbes' editors and reporters constantly bump into this bit by corporations—that they're in registration and cannot talk. The SEC has repeatedly assured *Forbes* that this is *not* so, that companies should be responsive to pertinent questions from the business press. There's a whale of a difference between attempting to plant stock-boosting propaganda and responding forthrightly to responsible reporters.

Sure, legal counsel will always say no or recommend doing nothing to a management when there's any possibility that doing or saying something could be remotely misconstrued. But a CEO is a CEO because he must make the final decision when faced with conflicting advice and fuzzy SEC directives.

It takes guts as well as brains to manage a major corporate effort. It should not take much of either to enable a man to tell the difference between relevant corporate truths and proscribed stock touting.

If the SEC has to clarify this ABC again, it should

promptly do so. Too many managements are interpreting the touting regulations as an excuse for doing and saying too little or nothing at all when investors are entitled to know what's going on.

2/1/71

For the second time this spring, New York Stock Exchange President Keith Funston has warned against the current tendency to play the numbers game with low-priced stocks and new issues.

We all know that it is all but impossible to save fools from their folly. As the old Russian proverb says: Do not try to teach a fool; as well try to cure the dead. Why, then, should Mr. Funston and other responsible Wall Streeters waste their breath? For a very simple reason: When the bubble bursts and thousands of people are hurt, it will not be enough for the financial community to say: "I told you so." Justly or unjustly, Wall Street is going to get blamed. And the companies whose stocks are involved also may suffer. As Mr. Funston said: "Every company wants serious owners—not people who are buying because a next-door neighbor passed on a vague tip from an uncertain source."

Therefore, it is incumbent on brokers and everyone connected with financing to do all they can to check the speculative mania that has seen stocks of new companies come out at 2 and go to 5 or even 10 in a few weeks. Probably, no one can force people to read carefully the prospectus. But at least the financial community can make it harder for the fools to act like fools.

6/1/61

If I owned any of these Hot New Issues that have doubled, tripled, quintupled, or umptupled within days and in some cases hours after they were issued, I most certainly would grab my fabulous windfall, thank my lucky stars, and then *invest* the money.

It's utter nonsense to think that overnight any newly issued stock is really worth two, ten, or twenty times the price both company and underwriters agreed upon as a fair market value. If this infinitely higher value is there, then a management so stupid as to sell shares at a fraction of their worth, and an underwriter so obtuse as not to discern the real value, together would provide reason enough for a sensible man to get rid of his shares.

I know the litany of Litton and Xerox and IBM as well as the next guy, but for each such rare case there are literally hundreds of others quite the reverse.

It's all well and good for today's men in charge to have only vague memories of the Depression. There is no excuse, however, for any but the freshest Wall Street freshman to have forgotten 1962.

If you were lucky enough—or, if you prefer, wise enough—to have secured shares of the recent Hots, I'd settle for having multiply multiplied my investment, and sell today. It's going to take a very long time for actual worth, actual growth, actual earnings to make such shares actually worth their present P/E.

10/15/67

Hold onto your hat.

Better yet, get out.

Out of those untested, wildly soaring, Hot New Issues, those over-the-counter IBMs of Tomorrow, whose most visible assets seem to be marketplace assets; out of stocks that have doubled, tripled, and quadrupled on little more than the greed of "sure-thing" grabbers.

You know the kind of stocks I'm talking about.

There's going to be, not necessarily too long from now,

a '62-like correction—punishment would be a better word—of the present market binge. The good stuff will no doubt suffer along with the bad, but nothing like as bad and not for very long.

This is the right time for those with undeserved, dizzy speculative profits to take 'em while they still got 'em.

To coin a phrase, nobody ever went broke taking a profit.

7/15/68

HOT NEW ISSUES

Balloons
  usually
    leak—
      or
      bust.

11/15/68

It's past time certified public accountants were called to account for practices that are so loose that they can be used to conceal rather than reveal a company's true financial picture.

The owners of public companies and the analysts who recommend purchase or sale of their securities used to think they could rely on the honesty of financial statements certified by reputable outside auditing firms. But in some very spectacular situations, it has turned out that such certification was not of the value or meaning or importance that the public thought. All these certifications usually bear the phrase: "according to generally accepted accounting principles," a phrase which is now coming to be generally accepted as damned meaningless.

When the Westec situation hit the fan, it developed that

the Ernst & Ernst certification was so "liberal" as to warrant a less flattering description.

Then, not long ago, there was the Yale Express case.

In a recent issue of *Forbes*, Leonard Spacek, chairman of Chicago's CPA firm of Arthur Andersen & Co., urged "the establishment of an official government court, appointed by the President, with jurisdiction over not only CPAs but also federal agencies like the Securities and Exchange Commission, Federal Power Commission, and Interstate Commerce Commission, to rule on accounting principles." With firm rulings from a government group, Spacek reasons, CPAs will not be subject, as they presently are, to client pressure.

Does he think the uproar over Westec's accounting practices will help bring about sweeping reform? Spacek shakes his head. "No, not unless the public demands it, as they did of the auto companies over the safety issue."

We do. Before government action is taken, the stock exchanges, industry groups, and CPAs themselves ought to get together to establish accounting standards that will be standard and a method of enforcement that will be enforceable.

10/15/66

It is never too late to make a New Year's resolution. With corporate annual report time around the corner, resolve this year to read the footnotes with greater avidity than the balance sheet. Often therein lies—buried—the real story of a company's year and yield.

If you don't understand or can't make sense out of the phraseology, that doesn't necessarily mean *you* are dumb. Only those who pretend they understand what they don't are thus fairly described.

When footnote phraseology clouds the point instead of clarifying it, write the report's signer asking if he could say what's meant in words that do so.

3/1/71

At Harvard Business School during the opening course in finance at the beginning of September 1929, Professor Deming drew stock market charts on the blackboard for his students and pointed out emphatically that it was absolutely impossible for stock market prices to remain anywhere near their then high prices.

Joseph V. Quarles, now president of Simmons Company, was recollecting this occasion for some of us the other day.

"Why didn't you pass the word to your father?" I queried.

Replied Mr. Quarles, "I did, in a sixteen-page letter. He dismissed the whole thing as typical college professor–impressionable student stuff."

"One week in business school and you're a stock market expert" was his fatherly reaction to his son's alarmed advice to sell.

10/15/72

Did you ever hear a man *with* money telling you how much he made betting on the horses?

It's invariably a man with no money who tells how much he makes betting on 'em.

Stock market speculators aren't gamblers. They're sure losers—with certain, if uncertain, fiscal interment dates.

4/15/73

Opinions on People

What more could anyone have asked of *any* President of the United States than Richard Nixon has accomplished in his first term?

I seriously doubt if any other President would have dared, had he the capability and vision, to have established a firm and real rapport with China, to have painstakingly arrived at a halt in the atomic arms race with Russia, to have effectively supported Israel's independence while pursuing a hopeful dialogue with Cairo for Middle East peace, to have removed virtually all American ground combat forces from Vietnam, and to have announced the end in a few months of the draft.

On the home front, no one would have believed that the inflation rate, so rapidly getting out of hand a couple of years ago, would have almost halved by now—with more people employed today than four years ago.

Of course, great and unsolved problems abound within our country and around the world.

Of course, many programs sought have failed passage; many administrative policies have come in for vehement criticism, some legitimate and some purely partisan.

Of course, President Nixon is criticized by many for his lack of Kennedy charisma and Eisenhower fatherliness.

But the number and magnitude of achievements in his first term dwarf those of any President since F.D.R. When he took office in 1969, many anticipated soundness in a Nixon Administration, but I doubt if anybody anticipated such greatness in terms of concrete accomplishments.

I really don't think fair-minded and reasonable people could have asked anything more of a President—or, in fact, anything like as much of a President—than Richard Nixon has delivered.

"Four More Years?" is the rhetorical query often heard these days. I believe and hope a sizable majority of us would reply, "We Hope So."

11/1/72

There are those who worry that the unprecedented magnitude of President Nixon's victory will have a dangerous effect on his head. It won't. It's apt to intoxicate for a bit some of those about him, but Richard Nixon has been through as tough, bitter, intensive, debilitating, exhilarating, disastrous, triumphant a public life as any man who's ever held the job, and this win won't affect his stride one iota.

The one place you won't find his head is in the clouds; the one place you won't find his feet is in quicksand.

What will the next four years bring?

He no more knows that than you or I.

But those who speculate that Richard Nixon will seek during the next four years some vague concept of Greatness, marbled Immortality, or lyrical, misty-eyed love and adoration from the *Washington Post* and *The New York Times* and the Fourth Estate might as well take up or give up smoking pot.

You see, about the only thing that this most press-dissected man of our time has never been accused of is meaning what he says.

But he does.

It's just that simple.

He really, honestly, and truly does believe in the verities of hard work and the efficacy of hard knuckles. He thinks we live in a hard world and that it takes a hard-headed approach to survive, to win, to stay out front, to stay on top, to stay with it, and—infinitely more preferable—to stay ahead of it.

Pundits are fond of listing the things and people Mr. Nixon is not—like Lincoln and Socrates and F.D.R. and God and Oliver Wendell Holmes and Joe Namath. But if you want to know what kind of man and President he's now going to be with this stupendous new mandate, I can give you an absolutely accurate answer—

Exactly the man and President he has been for the past four years.

And the election results rather emphatically indicate that's the sort of President most Americans want.

11/15/72

Zsa Zsa, Ltd., a twenty-four-month-old cosmetic outfit headed by the age-old Gabor herself, recently filed a Chapter 11 proceeding under the Federal Bankruptcy Act. At the time Gulf & Western was reportedly interested in buying the bag.

Commented Miss Hungary of 1936, with unconsciously devastating wit: "Nothing at all is wrong at our company. We need to reorganize the management and we need more money. I think we need a genius like Mr. Bluhdorn to do both things for us."

In that same interview Miss Gabor described her expensive cosmetics line as using "some old family secrets" from Hungary. The formula obviously must involve large quantities of that prevalent chemical formula—abbreviated as B.S.

11/1/70

In this time of ever-increasing tension, with survival of the human race at stake, I suppose we should be grateful for the diversion supplied by the asinine antics of two figures of fame, Field Marshal Viscount Montgomery and the Midnight Eminence of TV, Jack Paar.

What a pair! Here is Monty, Britain's popular wartime hero, traipsing off to Peiping to make the "startling" pronouncements to which nobody at home would pay any heed. It is really pathetic to watch a garrulous old man who had been a symbol of accomplishment for the British people as they held the fort for the free world during the last war, now advocating that the West buy peace by acquiescence to Communist demands. No one, least of all in Britain, pays much heed, but it is sad to see such aggressive senility in one who once meant something so different to the Allies of World War II.

Then there is Paar bravely prancing along the Berlin wall, fearlessly facing his TV tape while a large group of American G.I.s are engaged as props. As Paar is staging this pantomime, incidents of the tossing back and forth of water, rocks, and tear gas go on at the wall. Any one of them could in moments trigger the world explosion.

An incredible performance.

If Mr. Paar really wants to give his show an all-time rating he ought to hold a "summit conference" on it between Montgomery and himself. The results should indeed panic the world, and all doctors agree that laughter in a time of tension is very healthy.

10/1/61

"Maybe I'm worth $5 million a year."

That's what Harold Geneen said to *Forbes* when asked if he thought chief executive officers are paid too much. This unquestionable head of IT&T was the highest paid United States executive last year—$767,000.

"What do you pay somebody who has contributed $11 billion to his company?" Geneen asked, summing up the vast growth in his company's market value since he took it firmly into his no-nonsense hands twelve years ago. "Maybe if I study this hard enough I'll decide I'm worth $5 million a year and a lot of other guys around here are worth $2 million each."

At that point he quickly said he wasn't serious about paying himself that much.

Maybe he should be, though.

Maybe most stockholders would be better off if chief executives were paid as he suggests, "on the record," that is, a company's profitability and growth in stockholder equity and

market value. I quote further from that Geneen interview
with *Forbes*:

> It annoys Geneen that entrepreneurs who start companies
> and then sell them or take them public can end up with
> hundreds of millions of dollars. And taxed at capital gains
> rates, too. But the guy who actually runs a company isn't
> even in the same league. "We bought," he says of IT&T,
> "roughly 100 companies from individuals or closely held
> groups and paid anywhere from $500,000 to $100 million
> for each. For example, no one gets excited when we pay,
> say, $50 million to buy a company and the entrepreneur
> gets that amount for, say, fifteen years' work, all lightly
> taxed. Stockholders don't get excited because you can
> measure what a *company* is worth.
>
> "But that guy who sold it probably managed maybe
> 1,000 people at the most. We're managing 400,000 people.
> And we have the finest record in the country. On a com-
> pound basis, our rate of growth in earnings per share is
> 11.6 percent, second only to IBM among big companies."
>
> Considering this accomplishment, considering what
> some entrepreneurs are paid for lesser accomplishments,
> Geneen wonders why anyone would question his salary.
> "Let me tell you a true story. I've just sold part of this
> little business I own [Acme Visible Records] and made
> more money out of that than I've ever made out of IT&T.
> And I did that with one-tenth of 1 percent of my time."
>
> Geneen feels one of the problems is that as a pro-
> fessional manager, shareholders feel you work for them.
> They wonder why anyone who is working for them makes
> more than the shareholders do themselves. Apparently,
> they see nothing wrong with a capitalist or an entre-
> preneur or an inheritor making or gaining fortunes.

For a good many years *Forbes* has carried shares of
IT&T in our retirement and thrift plans. From time to time
we've bought additional shares. Almost invariably, our in-

vestment committee's only regret, each time we made a new purchase, was that we hadn't bought more shares sooner.

As stockholders, we'd much rather see the Geneens who CEO our corporate holdings paid $2 million or $3 million a year to keep on compounding our shares' earnings and value than to lose such men to some wee capital-gains entrepreneurship.

By any yardstick the salary of a Geneen is relatively minuscule per each ever more valuable share. Geneen's $767,-000 was equal to about seven-tenths of a cent per IT&T common share. If accomplishment in profitable corporate growth is the yardstick, I wish there were a couple of hundred more like him to collect ceilingless salaries.

8/1/71

Betting on "Rapid" Riklis
may be more reckless than riskless.

3/15/72

Howard Morgens is one of the Quiet Big Ones with a brainy, total grasp of what management really is and means. As the determinedly unsung CEO of Procter & Gamble for the past decade and a half, he's stayed way on top of one of the most toughly competitive businesses in the world. In a backgrounder luncheon here the other day, Mr. Morgens made one observation on developing managerial ability in young men that I asked to quote:

"Put younger men in jobs *before* they're ready. Then don't let them make mistakes until they're ready."

2/15/72

The oil industry ought to lubricate some of its squeaking spokesmen.

Not long ago Chicago's oil Napoleon, John Swearingen,

head of Standard Oil of Indiana, was reported in *The New York Times* as having "acknowledged the seriousness of the pollution problem. But he also attacked what he called 'hysteria' and indirectly criticized the General Motors Corporation, which is pressing the antipollution fight from Detroit."

He said less-polluting gasoline would, on the average, cost more.

So?

Let's lay off General Motors, John, and get the lead out. I'm sure if you will do your thing, as General Motors is doing theirs with depollution projects, we will all live a little longer.

5/15/70

Now that Mr. Burns has been seated as chairman of the Federal Reserve with a full quota of hopeful hoopla, and William McChesney Martin has been retired under a deserved avalanche of encomiums, we'd just like to add this postscript. The praises for Retiring William often took on the ring of eulogies. *Forbes* would like to point out that the man ain't dead, and I hope he's not foolish enough to bury himself under some inappropriate notion that silence is now his proper lot.

Such modesty is an unheard of trait among economists generally, especially by those who have ample to be modest about. In the first press of the Press for reminiscences and ruminations by Mr. Martin, he has vigorously shied away. Even *Forbes* couldn't yet pry him into submitting to quotatable probes.

After a suitable period and at an appropriate time and place though, he should speak up, speak out. His views will no longer help to make official policy per se, so inner sanctum secrecy is no longer a required tool of his trade. His background and his thinking remain valuable, and his right to silence is strictly short term.

William, in the course of not too much time, you must be heard.

If your words are not always heeded in their entirety, it won't be the first time.

You continue to have an important part to play; it's just a bit different.

7/1/70

Not long ago Seagram President Edgar Bronfman, whose father controls the outfit, told a *Forbes* reporter: "I think that anybody can make it on his own. The hard thing is to inherit it."

That Wilde-like witticism is, you know, profoundly true.

My father used to say the same thing in other words: "The hardest thing in the world is for a rich man's son to amount to anything." In Dad's time, and by his definition, amounting to anything meant succeeding in business. Today, I think most Americans would allow that amounting to something can be done in a somewhat wider spectrum.

The point, however, remains valid.

When you remove the very elementary need to earn a living, to work, you have taken away the most basic motivation. To rev up your motor when you don't even have to get up any morning you don't want to is difficult.

Doing what you have to do is hard enough for most of us. Doing what you don't have to do is even harder.

Lots of us, despite the difficulty, would like to try our hand at it, though.

1/1/66

At a luncheon *Forbes'* editors had here a while back with North American's [now Rockwell International] CEO, Al Rockwell, I mentioned that it was quite unusual for the son of an extraordinary achiever such as his father, Colonel Rockwell, to become such an extraordinary achiever himself.

He commented that "I have always heard that if the son isn't abler than the father, there's something wrong with either the son or the father.

"I have worked like blazes all my life to prove there's nothing wrong with my old man."

And succeeded, I might add.

6/15/72

Private Donald Till was being transported to a court-martial by the army. There are a couple of hundred assorted charges against him, including AWOL. Obviously, the army considered him a bad actor.

Bad actor?

He was being flown in a small army plane to the stockade at Fort Riley, Kansas, and this character who has been bucking the whole military machine for months persuaded his guards that he was so afraid of flying that he wanted to wear a parachute.

They fell for it, and shortly after takeoff he popped out of the plane and floated to temporary freedom.

Instead of being a bad actor, I'd say he was a pretty good one.

Instead of sticking him in the pokey, I think the army ought to make him a captain in the Special Forces where gall, gumption, get-up-and-go are prized.

For his wile and will, let's form the Society for the Promotion of Till.

3/15/69

Scientists have concluded that the raging brush fires we so desperately fight and deplore are actually beneficial.

California biologist Carl Baker opines that "We will have ten times as many animals within a decade in the burned areas as before the fires. The watershed will be greatly enhanced. Vast recreation areas which have been closed in the past will be open for people to enjoy." Adds biology Professor Philip Miller: "About ten years ago ecologists recognized fire as a natural ecological process. . . . Indians intentionally set fires throughout recorded history."

Whatever will become of dear old Smokey the Bear now that he will be joining the ranks of the unemployed?

8/15/71

Bill Buckley, that Righter of Wronged Rightists, is again a candidate for office, this time for trustee of his alma mater —Yale.

You can bet your boots he wasn't nominated by the nominating committee of alumni leaders, who invariably present a slate that includes three unvarying varieties—an antiseptic Chipsian intellectual; an impeccable, prominent industrialist or lawyer, preferably wealthly; and some little-knowner who has struggled long and faithfully raising money and reunion attendance in a valiant effort to preserve Class and class.

Yale's alumni this spring will have a different choice.

Buckley got himself on the Yale ballot by using a never-used clause permitting nomination by petition—a proviso provided only to maintain the desirable fiction of democratic process.

Mr. Buckley runs as part of his lifelong effort to re-establish the disestablished Establishment.

His platform will probably prove irresistibly alluring to a majority of Yale alumni. He protests the university's broadened admissions policy and its "liberal imbalance. . . .

All other qualifications being equal, the son of the Yale alumnus should have preference over the son of a nonalumnus." He says that Yale has become "distinctly and observably hostile to the conservative point of view."

Admits the testy, teasing TV star of Buckley's *Firing Line*, "it's considered infra-dig to campaign for this sort of thing." The Yale nominators were so undone at the prospects of this Voice of Reaction being heard at meetings of the Yale Corporation that they prevailed upon one of their most brilliant sons to go on the ballot in opposition: Cyrus R. Vance, troubleshooter par excellence for President Johnson, former Under Secretary of Defense, and presently a key figure on the American team now negotiating in Paris over Vietnam.

Observed Mr. Buckley: "I'm sure Mr. Vance is a very nice man and I hope that he will be more successful against me than he has been against the Vietcong, but my guess is that I probably will win."

It would be a crying shame if Mr. Vance's candidacy is wasted because he would be a trustee of inestimable value to any outfit.

On the other hand, you must admit it would be also of inestimable value to the Yale Corporation to have one voice of its eighteen heard expressing the too-long-unheard cries of the Undefended and Indefensibles.

6/1/68

Art Buchwald, in the opinion of hundreds of thousands of us, is one of the greatest scriveners of our times. His satire is devastating but done gently; always humorously, never savagely. His humor is never of the big-guffaw, "Have you heard this one?" variety. Rather it is penetrating, witty, with point and purpose.

These orchids to the irreverent Mr. Buchwald spring

from seeing him the other night at a restaurant. He didn't see me and, if he had, wouldn't have remembered me anyway. But I'll never forget how he once removed my then-young legs right out from under me.

In 1951 I flew to Paris with a suitcase full of petitions urging Ike to become a candidate for the Republican presidential nomination. Art Buchwald was then doing his famous column for the Paris *Herald Tribune*, and his New York boss was one of those who paved my way to General Eisenhower's sacrosanct nonpolitical SHAPE headquarters.

I had a telephone call from the columnist inviting me to lunch with him. I was most impressed, and I had visions of being featured in one of his articles.

We had what I thought was a delightful session, and I bent the Buchwald ear with all manner of brilliant observations, bons mots, and what have you about Ike, Paris, the Economy, and Me. I concluded to myself that one Buchwald column couldn't do me justice; I was sure I had poured out at least a week's worth of Buchwald.

About an hour and four wines later Mr. Buchwald stood up and said good-bye. "I don't like to run off so abruptly, but Zsa Zsa Gabor is in town, and I've got a chance to interview her. You know how it is—a writer is always on the lookout for usable copy."

I stayed on and finished the dregs of the wine.

8/1/64

As the nation mires ever faster, ever deeper into the most controversial war we've ever waged, many of the President's critics grow more unrestrained, more vitriolic, more vituperative. Even without a war, in an election year political partisanship often leads to a type of criticism that demeans the utterers more than their objective.

How well I remember the unbelievable extent to which the wife and family of Franklin D. Roosevelt were subjected to abuse, particularly from the beginning of his second term until Pearl Harbor. It is a pretty shabby footnote in our history.

As the bitterness of war and the election grows, I hope we do not again behave in such a crummy and juvenile way toward the President's family.

It is quite aside from the point, but a point well worth making anyway, that we are most fortunate that the First Lady of this land is such a dedicated, gracious, and caring lady. She has made a most positive contribution at a high cost of time and effort to many problem areas, such as conservation and beautification. The evident sincerity of her interest in people struggling with urban poverty is inspiring.

Mrs. Johnson doesn't *have* to put her neck out or expose herself to the slings and arrows. She has done so with tact and conviction and results.

And I guess even the Johnsons' most fervent critics have given them full points for the way their attractive daughters have behaved under the enormous disadvantages of their great advantages.

Possibly these observations don't really have much place in a magazine of business. Yet keeping some perspective on what after all are some of the real values in life is always relative—be you businessman or politician or whatever, or however vehemently you feel.

3/15/68

Henry Kissinger may not be able to walk on water, but he is doing the nearest thing to it since it was first done.

When he was named for the Nobel Peace Prize, many

with emotional unthinkingness were surprised, shocked, de-
risive. He not only deserves the Nobel award for past performance, but the next Nobel for his present performance.

Anyway, anyone with the wit to express the wistful wish
for a plane "with a detachable press compartment" in which
to do his constant globe-trotting has to be a winsome winner.

1/15/74

The President's appointment of former Texas Governor
John Connally as Secretary of the Treasury came as a total
surprise. It's as unlikely a pick as one could imagine.

And, contrary to prevalent opinion, I think Mr. Connally could turn out to be one of the most effective men to
hold the job in recent decades. The first-blush premise that
the naming of a nationally known, effective Texas Democrat
was for purely and obvious political reasons is wrong. Once
again commentators underestimate Richard Nixon's hard-
headed good sense.

With Vietnam disengagement proceeding apace, only a
worsening recession will dump the Republicans out of the
White House in the election that will be taking place twenty-
one months from now. One has to be unthinking or dumb to
conclude that the President selected his Treasury Secretary
to help carry Texas when unsolving the problems facing the
Treasury could cost the GOP both Texas and the nation at
the next national polls.

This Administration has a good stable of high-caliber
economics professorial Shultz-McCracken types, and can well
use a political and highly experienced Business Hard Hat to
keep theory related to reality, and to get Administration
measures through Congress.

In addition to having immense respect from respected
legislators on Capitol Hill, Secretary-to-be Connally has had

enough experience both from his tour as Naval Secretary and his highly successful terms as Texas Governor to make the Treasury bureaucracy perform as directed. That's no small skill, because inertia in bureaucratic ranks short-circuits more executive directives than ever did the Congress or the press or anyone else.

As a matter of fact, ticking off Connally as simply a successful politico overlooks his real business savvy and extensive experience. As a lawyer he has been an active director with Houston's outstanding First City National Bank and a trustee of the venerable, estimable U.S. Trust Company of New York; a director of that first-rate outfit Halliburton Company; as well, a director of Texas Instruments, Inc.; and he has been active on the President's Advisory Council on Executive Organization.

Enjoying the President's confidence and having a lot of confidence—with reason—of his own, Treasury Secretary Connally will be heard respectfully and effectively in international councils and pack some real wallop in White House councils and on Capitol Hill.

In short, for a lot of unobvious reasons, this Texan in the Treasury at a time of economic stress is good.

Very good.

1/15/71

All of us who work at the business of business can take some comfort and confidence from the fact that George Shultz now counsels the President on a par with Messrs. Mitchell, Ehrlichman, and Kissinger.

His approach is pragmatic rather than dogmatic, dogged not docile in pursuit of policies and programs he deems sound and sensible.

Incidentally, he had these qualities as a very young

youngster. We grew up together in Englewood, New Jersey. I found then his tenacity at schoolwork a bit of a pain in the neck. Then—at eight and nine and ten years old—as now, I didn't like working harder than necessary. George, by dint of digging until he had mastered the arithmetic lesson or the geography homework, kept making it necessary for all the rest of us to try harder if we were to get decent marks.

On Friday evenings five of us, including George, would traipse a mile and a half to neighboring homes after our Boy Scout troop meeting. Time and again he would dampen our enthusiasm for some un-Scoutlike mischief. When he couldn't talk us out of it, he would disassociate himself from the scene and stoically go on his way. At twelve and thirteen and fourteen, that takes more determination than perhaps is now recollectible.

It isn't every Secretary of Labor who would have the courage to urge companies to take strong positions against high wage settlements even if it means a strike. Not long ago, Labor Secretary Shultz did just that: "We can't make industrial peace our sole and main objective in collective bargaining. . . . While I'm not saying the strike is desirable, the peaceful strike is probably one of the least worst forms of protest we know. . . . Union leaders cannot take the position that their members should not be asking for high wage increases. That's got to come from management, and if there are no people who take that position, we will never be able to solve these [inflation] problems."

When George Shultz has them, the presidential ears will be in good hands.

7/15/70

Colorful outspokenness is not the hallmark of high-ups in the Nixon Administration—er, that is, since Martha left.

Though he's publicly almost never outspoken, the President's truculent top Prussian, John D. Ehrlichman, is widely known inside Washington for his asperity toward the press and any other Administration critic. Recently, though, on a TV show he uncorked a couple of beautiful haymakers for the Fourth Estate, which doesn't seem to march often enough to the Ehrlichman cadence. Asked why the President holds so few news conferences, Adviser John explained that the President considers conference questions to be "flabby and fairly dumb. I've seen him many times come off one of those things and say, 'Isn't it extraordinary how poor the quality of the questions is?'" He went on to compare the press present at press conferences to "insecure young ladies—they keep asking us if we love them. If you don't want to know, don't ask."

Isn't it good to have someone else in the Administration capable of colorful new Marthaisms!

8/1/72

To lure the Women's Lib vote, maybe Nixon's top aides, Messrs. Ehrlichman and Haldeman, should change their names to Ehrlichperson and Haldeperson?

11/1/72

Poor Kennedy.

I don't mean Teddy.

I'm talking about David.

If he didn't already have a bundle of his own and wasn't making a pretty good salary as head of the mint, he could make a mintful more on the circuit, billed as the Only Man Who Can Stand Up With Both Feet In His Mouth—And Talk.

After the Treasury Secretary on previous occasions sug-

gested the possibility of wage and price controls to curb
inflation, a presidential spokesman for Richard M. Nixon let
it be known there was absolutely no such prospect or plans
by his administration.

Recently, the Redoubtable David said it again, and again
the presidential spokesman said baloney. Secretary Kennedy
further confounded the White House by describing the rise
in unemployment to 4 percent as "acceptable." Said he,
"There's no question, as you slow the economy, there will be
some increases in unemployment."

One of these days he'll learn that telling the truth is
sometimes—ofttimes—inappropriate for a man in power.

11/1/69

AGNEW

Tragic is what the charitable would say.
Incredible is more descriptive.

11/1/73

It's a hazardous thing for commentators to name contemporaries who will figure importantly in future histories of our
time. But I am as certain as a man can be that the present
Chief Justice will be written about as one of the small handful of Milestone Men whose names mark singularly important
events in the history of our courts and our country.

Why?

Because he has a simple, essential, nearly unachievable
goal in mind, and I think over a reasonable period of time
this genially canny, judicially determined man will accom-
plish it. He aims to see our present court system—state and
federal—restructured so that a judge can judge, so that those
involved in civil or criminal proceedings can have a "fair,
honest, and speedy determination of issues."

Liberty is an abstract concept without Justice, and there can be little justice when the time of decision ranges from indefinite to infinite.

Two Warren Burger qualities will make possible a substantial achievement of this goal. In the first place, he is not as awed by the awesomeness of his great office as much as he is aware of its limitations, its powerlessness to dictate. His leadership can only be made effective by persistent persuasion; unremitting, unheadlined effort; encouragement and education of those who can do what needs doing.

Secondly, this long-practicing lawyer knows where to begin, what needs to be done or tried or changed, and his approach is on a brick-by-brick basis. Begin with little steps, first things first, because no singular spectacular thing will produce the miracle.

I believe that in time, under this man's leadership, "Justice for all" will become much more of a reality for us all.

7/1/71

When David Packard, helmsman of the eminently successful electronics company Hewlett-Packard, was named by President Nixon to the key post of Deputy Defense Secretary, he was an unknown quantity to most of the country.

At his retirement from that post and his return to chairmaning the Hewlett-Packard board three years after leaving it, I doubt if any informed and caring citizen isn't mighty sorry to see him go. He was able to bring order and sense to the incredibly vast and complicated defense procurement procedures.

The country reaped an additional dividend from his service. His holdings in Hewlett-Packard were put in trust with the understanding that if there were any profits and dividends, all would go to charity on his separation from government. It turns out there was $23 million worth.

While there are not many in a position to give up $23 million for the privilege of working interminable hours in one of the country's toughest jobs for a salary of $42,500 a year, it's nice to know that one who could, did.

David Packard's a good man.

1/15/72

I certainly hope Defense Secretary Robert S. NcNamara isn't as impervious to criticism or as oblivious to suggestion as his critics imply. With equal fervor I hope his innards are not as sensitive as the computing machines to which he is often likened. In recent weeks he must be wondering what's hit him. From every side and from some of the most unlikely sources, he has been attacked and assaulted not merely for his conclusions and actions; his *motives* in addition to his methods have been keelhauled.

I hope he can take it because I share what I feel is still a widely held opinion that he is the ablest Defense Secretary we've had and the ablest man on the Kennedy team.

Nobody making decisions that involve both the placing and canceling of billions of dollars in contracts affecting tens of thousands of people's jobs and income can expect to win popularity contests. But such decisions have to be made and that's the Defense Secretary's job. It's heartening to find out that the Defense Secretary doesn't view his task as one of trying to keep the army, navy, and air force happy in equal parts regardless of technical development and changing defense needs.

I don't know whether he made a mistake on the TFX contract. I don't know if getting one plane for the army and the navy at a savings of hundreds of millions of dollars is worth the saving. I always thought planes were built in relation to missions as well as costs, that perhaps carrier-based planes might have different requirements than land-based, etcetera.

Etcetera.

Etcetera.

Etcetera.

But if I, who ain't in the business, have these thoughts; and if some congressmen have them; and if some army, navy, and air force people have them; and if you have them—isn't it perhaps reasonable to suppose that they might have occurred to Mr. McNamara also?

As for the criticism repeatedly emanating from generals and admirals that he doesn't always follow their recommendations—good lord!

Mr. McNamara isn't God. He has no claim to infallibility. I'm sure he has made and will make mistakes. I hope and believe he listens to criticism.

I repeat, however, the fervent hope that he is not getting unduly rocked inside by the pummeling he has been undergoing. He is doing a well-nigh undoable job and doing it ably. After undergoing so many weeks of nonadulation I think it's time some of us in McNamara's band strike up for him an encouraging tune.

5/1/63

Ever since President Johnson took the oath of office last November, Americans by the millions have speculated about his choice of a running mate this November. Toward the end of this month, the game will be over, the selection made.

Who will it be?

Your guess is as good as mine—and vice versa. I strongly doubt if the President himself has as yet made his final decision.

Increasingly often at the top of the most "informed"

guess list is the name of Senator Hubert Humphrey (Dem., Minn.). If not the speculators' first possibility, he is usually number two, almost never lower than third.

What sort of a man is this whom fate or the march of time could well make the next President of the United States?

I found him to be in fact considerably more than the man I thought he was. Articulate, not glib; principled, not preachy; determined, not dogmatic; a man with an ebullient, deep-down faith in the goodness of his fellows, a faith apparently untarnished by the cynicism that inevitably accompanies success in politics.

His liberalism is real but not wild-eyed or far-out. He obviously no longer believes, if he early did, in push-button legislative solutions to complex problems.

Fascinatingly enough, he is at once a favorite of the Adlai Stevenson spectrum and increasingly one of the favorite senators of informed businessmen. In talking with a *Forbes* reporter about Humphrey, New York Stock Exchange President Keith Funston said, "If I had to name one of a half dozen people in Washington who would have been against us, Hubert Humphrey would have been at the head of the list. But I found out a couple of years ago he was a real capitalist. The business community had the wrong picture of him."

About the improving climate between business and government, Humphrey says this: "I am not for monopolies or price fixing, everybody knows that. But that kind of stuff isn't good for business either. I think the day of harassment of business by government is over. . . . For years business has looked on government as a natural enemy, that's fading now. . . . I think you have to have a favorable political climate to have a good economic climate."

Last week I flew to the Chicago Club to be present when

Senator Humphrey met and spoke off the record with two dozen of the country's topmost business leaders, gathered by Sears, Roebuck President Crowdus Baker. I was amazed to see General Robert Wood present and told him so. This venerable Curmudgeon of the Right, his eyes twinkling, quickly set me straight. "I am just back from the San Francisco convention. It was the greatest I ever attended. We finally fixed you Easterners! Why am I here? I'm thrilled with Barry Goldwater, but if Johnson *should* be reelected, I'd feel safer with Hubert Humphrey as Vice-President."

This onetime chief of Sears went on: "I disagree with most of his ideas, but if fate put him in the White House, I could go to sleep knowing we had on the job an honest man who truly loves his country."

The great difference between the Hubert Humphrey who entered the Senate sixteen years ago and the Hubert Humphrey who, with a couple of others, runs the Senate today is simply summarized: While his liberal convictions have not melted, he himself has mellowed, matured.

"If I believe in something," he says, "I will fight for it with all I have. But I do not demand all or nothing.

"Professional liberals want the fiery debate," says he. "They glory in defeat. A sort of political masochism. The hardest job for a politician today is to have the courage to be a moderate. It is easy to take an extreme position."

After the Chicago confab, I flew to Washington with the Minnesotan and four of his young aides. They were a happy, bright, believing group. Obviously dedicated to their boss, they clearly felt his future and theirs indeed lay ahead—just ahead. Come August 24 and then November 3, they could turn out to be quite right.

At least that's the way it looks to this Republican.

8/1/64

Never mind Sunday.

Why bother on Monday. Or Tuesday. Or Wednesday.
Or Thursday. Or Friday. Or Saturday.

I am talking about George Romney, who recently told
reporters, "I never talk politics on Sunday." So if he becomes
President, who in 'ell runs the country on Sunday? If a man
can deadpan such a sanctimonious, silly statement, who needs
him the other six days?

The fact is Governor Romney as a presidential possibility doesn't turn me on. It's conceivable, of course, that he's
brighter, better informed than many of his public words
would, so far, suggest. For instance, this climactic gobbledy-
gook from an NAM speech: "You, as national and local
leaders, are best qualified to innovate, initiate and organize the
political, social and economic action necessary to strengthen
the root sources of total problem-solving action in America
and thus preserve America as the 'last best hope of earth.'"

On another matter of some little interest to the American
people, our white-topped Rambler offers these observations on
the war in Vietnam: "I have been following it as closely as a
man can follow it in the position I've been in. And I've been
there. I've had briefings and I've read and I've talked with
people outside of this nation who have had experience closest
to ours, and I just want to say to you that I'm profoundly
concerned about the situation in South Vietnam."

It further bugs me when a man parades his piety. Like
when Mr. Romney let it be known he had communed with
God for several days before deciding whether to be a candidate for governor in Michigan the first time.

Then there's the transparent untruth. Like when immediately after last November's election, Gorgeous George and
Rocky vacationed in Puerto Rico and Our Boy, following a
one and a half hour conference with the New York Governor,

announced to the press that "this meeting is purely coincidence."

Nor does petulance at this early stage strike me as a prime essential for Presidents. Like when the man from Michigan teed off on reporters who had smoked out one of his unannounced politicking trips to New York: "I told you fellows straight out several weeks ago that I'm not going to tell you about every appointment or every trip I make. And I'll tell you why: There are too many political anthropologists who proceed to place a political interpretation on things they don't justify."

Maybe it's unfair to judge a man by his own verbal flap-doodle, but Harry Truman made it clear that ringing, syntactical rhetoric wasn't necessary for a President to be able to say what he thought.

If and when he did.

To sum it all up, I have a sinking feeling that Mr. Romney is floundering for a way to convey convictions he doesn't have, for solutions to problems that either don't exist, of if they exist, that he doesn't understand. The more he talks, the less he says.

In 1920 a handsome Republican wheel from the Midwest, who said nothing and said it convincingly, was swept into the presidency as the result of wide public ire with the incumbent Democratic Administration.

The 1968 similarities are startling, the prospects of a repetition of 1920 disturbing.

The new Lochinvar has another name, of course.

And I am sure his friends are honest.

But this is no time for another, albeit cronyless, Harding in the White House.

2/1/67

Wilbur Mills is the greatest.

Almost single-handedly last year and for many years before that, this Arkansas Congressman, chairman of the House Ways and Means Committee, has prevented the Big Spenders from spending us broke, and has kept a varied lot of Egotistical Economy Experts from expertising us into chaos.

This principal bastion of common sense is at the same time a warm, fair, good man. The other day, Ideal Basic Industries helmsman Cris Dobbins told me the experience a friend recently had with the redoubtable Mills. As he had in each of the Congressman's campaigns, the gentleman sent in his $100 contribution toward Mr. Mills' election expenses.

The check was returned with a "Thank you" and this sentence: "Since this year I had no opposition, I had no expenses."

I hope it is ever thus for Wilbur Mills.

He's the best thing that's happened to Capitol Hill since Robert Taft.

9/1/71

THE NEW stASSen
IS A DEMOCRAT
The name's now McCarthy.

2/1/72

In recent months I have had occasion to be in London several times and am happy to report that, despite difficulties and differences between Washington and London on numbers of things, there is a growing warmth, affection, and respect by the British people for President Nixon's ambassador to the Court of St. James, Walter Annenberg.

You may recall that at the outset Mr. Annenberg was

subject to unusual and sometimes vituperative criticism for a number of irrelevent or frivolous or political reasons. As time has passed and the Ambassador has had time to make his mark and do his job in his way, he has begun to win a valued spot in the regard of the reserved British.

The American business community will and should be very glad of it. This growing rapport is of inestimable value during this difficult time of tense negotiation in world trade.

2/1/71

Britain's Prince Philip is really quite a character, one of Britain's most valuable assets—at least when he's abroad. When not Consorting, he travels much and, all too often, so far as he's concerned, is called on for a few words.

These are often choice, for this court jester is a man of wit and keenness. To wit, this observation when some time ago a Paraguayan dictator dinnered him: "It's a pleasant change to be in a country which isn't ruled by its people."

Even his countrymen, famed for their non-sense of humor, enjoyed the chuckles that spread round the world; in fact, for the next couple of days they laid off their favorite preoccupation of belaboring their Prince.

As the Aussies would put it: Good on you, Philip, old boy!

3/15/67

The Empire is gone.

The hereditary Lords are about to be de-Housed.

Indeed, things ain't wot they used to be in Great Britain.

But, damn it, George Brown is just too bloody much.

For centuries British statesmen have wielded enormous influence quite above and beyond purely military capability. Knowledge, long experience of men and affairs, background, and intelligence—all were brought better to play on the international scene by the British.

What a travesty to that tradition is the present Foreign Secretary.

Britain no longer wields a very big stick in world affairs.

But they've got the biggest mouth on the scene.

And the trouble is, even with both his feet permanently in it, you can still understand what George Brown says.

It's usually garbage—liquid.

11/15/67

HAROLD WILSON

Who would ever have thought to see a once Prime Minister of Great Britain descend to less than the least among the people he at one time led.

3/15/72

When *Forbes* subscriber labels went from stencils onto computer rolls, the Secretary of State's address appeared as "2201 C Street, Washington, D.C. 20520."

The *Forbes* issue so addressed came back with a sticker next to the address headed: UNDELIVERABLE.

And the box marked "Moved—Left no address" was checked.

Now, where in the world do you suppose he has gone?

6/15/70

The universal sadness and the warmth of tributes that came forth throughout the land at Herbert Hoover's passing contrast vividly with the scorn in which he was held by millions when he went out of office in the depths of the Depression.

It took much time for people to become generally aware that he was neither the cause of nor had he the power to cure that devastating economic collapse.

I have in front of me a poignant letter that he wrote my father twenty-two years ago. Dad had asked him to head up a nationwide organization of stockholders to protect investors from political abuse.

Mr. Hoover replied:

> Stanford University
> California
> April 8, 1942

Dear Mr. Forbes:

I have your letter of April 3.

I have too much else on my mind at the moment to undertake the matter which you suggest. Somebody ought to do it, but perhaps someone who is not so *persona non grata* as I am.

> Yours faithfully,
> Herbert Hoover

Isn't it a happy thing that this great citizen lived long enough to find himself esteemed and loved by virtually all Americans? He had to live a long time for it to happen, but the good Lord gave him and us enough time.

11/1/64

Three and a half years ago I worked hard for the election of Richard Nixon to the Presidency, and as a delegate of the GOP Convention happily voted for his nomination. During the Democratic Convention I rooted for Lyndon B. Johnson in the conviction expressed often to friends that, "If a Democrat should win, he'd be the best one." Kennedy? Too young, too inexperienced. Attractive, eager, but not mature enough.

At lunch with two friends forty-eight hours before President Kennedy's death, we discussed at length how glad we were that he was President; that in foreign affairs, American objectives, hopes, and ideals had been made clear and had been kept clear; that the President had displayed firmness without resorting to shallow and explosive brinksmanship. We commented on how no Republican President probably would have dared to ask for the tax reduction so necessary to our maximum economic expansion.

We rounded out the conversation by concluding that Kennedy would undoubtedly be reelected and that by the end of his second term he would be considered as one of the handful of great Presidents.

In thirty-six months there are few specific legislative milestones on which historians can peg an evaluation of President Kennedy's Administration, but his greatness as a man is firmly established. With wit and wisdom and calmness he met world crises, and continually concerned himself with measures that would benefit the human lot.

On these pages *Forbes* in past months has on several occasions supported his actions and proposals.

The man is now beyond support, but some of the measures and the need of them remain.

What now? What about Lyndon Johnson?

I can recollect no unelected—and few elected Presidents —who have come into office with better preparation for the job. In the three most immediate problems facing the country, President Johnson had unusual responsibilities under John Kennedy.

He was knee-deep in defense problems, particularly in matters of space.

In the field of civil rights, he headed the President's Committee on Equal Employment Opportunity.

In connection with foreign relations, he has in recent months acquired firsthand familiarity with most of our allies and friends abroad.

Before this exposure to national responsibility on the

executive level, he, in title and in fact, led the legislative branch as Majority Leader of the Senate. Virtually every important legislative measure during President Eisenhower's last six years achieved passage primarily because of Johnson's help. His support of foreign aid and trade, NATO and the UN, Social Security, and expanded civil rights is a matter of record, both in words and deeds.

In one very significant area, Johnson's skill exceeds that of the late President—how to get things through Congress.

President Johnson displays one attitude strikingly similar to President Eisenhower's: an almost fervent belief in the free enterprise system. Anybody tempted to sell securities because of uncertainty about the new Administration should listen to a replay of the Texas TV station's interview with the President and Mrs. Johnson at the L.B.J. Ranch, recorded a few weeks ago. No Republican, no conservative, no business leader, no Vermont Yankee ever gave greater or more continuous expression of conviction about free enterprise and the "American way" of economic life than the new President of the United States.

In our profound misfortune we are fortunate that the new hand at the helm is an experienced, firm one. President Johnson knows unusually well the process of governing and the problems facing the government. He knows unusually well men in government and particularly the men now in his government.

In despairing over the still unbelievable deed of assassination, we certainly need not despair over our country's present leadership and future prospects.

12/1/63

A couple of weeks ago I presented Robert Kennedy to a small group gathered at a Washington luncheon to support establishment of a modest domestic peace corps. When President Kennedy first made the creation of a national service corps part of his program seven months before his death, the Attorney General became a prime mover in the effort for its passage.

At this most recent meeting, he spoke quietly, with simplicity. After briefly cataloging the merits of the measure, he outlined with little emotion, but very realistically, the difficulties facing the bill in the House. The talk itself was effective. But I was more deeply affected by the quite extraordinary change in the man himself since the murder of his brother.

During the pre-convention primaries, at the convention itself, during the presidential campaign, and in the early months of the Kennedy Administration, I thoroughly shared the rather widely held opinion that brother Bobby was brilliant, brash, tough, vindictive. He was the man who kept the old score cards on Who Was For Kennedy Before Los Angeles; the presidential follow-through, get-things-done man; chief of the White House Irish Mafia. In short, the villain of any Kennedy Administration piece that antagonized anyone. Like Cuba. Like the steel price rollback if you were a businessman. Or civil rights if you were a Southerner. Or indictments if you were Hoffa.

On these pages I found a number of occasions to support warmly many acts and actions of President Kennedy. But to keep my franchise as a Registered Republican, I managed to get in my licks at younger brother.

I had had only the most passing personal contacts with Robert Kennedy, when some of us met with him in the Justice Department to map support for the National Service Corps six months ago. Our discussions then simply reconfirmed the impression of brilliance, but added a new dimension that I hadn't before suspected in the man. There was great candor and keen, witty awareness. Said the Attorney General: "This bill probably faces additional difficulties in the House because my personal enthusiasm for it seems to generate the opposite effect on a number of southern congressmen. I also seem to have limited powers of persuasion with most Republican congressmen. Since we need some votes from each group to pass the bill, those of you who see its merits, regardless of politics, will have to do the selling on Capitol Hill."

The fact that what he said was true didn't impress me quite as much as the fact that he recognized his limitations. At the relatively young age of thirty-eight, when a man is the second most powerful figure in the United States by virtue of his total rapport with the President, it's rather easy not to recognize limitations in power or personality.

But the man of two weeks ago is not the same man of four months ago. The gaunt look is etched deep. I doubt that it will pass with time. The fire and fervor and drive that come from spectacular success and power of worldwide consequence is visibly gone. Shock and disbelief seem still evident in this yet young, but no longer youthful man. There is no trace of sourness or bitterness or frustration in him. His keen perception and sharp judgment about people and power and method and measure are not less than they were but perhaps deeper, broader than before. Not dulled, but perhaps leavened by a greater degree of "the milk of human kindness."

Robert Kennedy's future? I don't for a minute believe he will be picked as President Johnson's running mate. Before Dallas they were not swimming-pool-dunking buddies.

On the contrary, I do not believe either that the Attorney General after the election will find for very long any sense of happiness or accomplishment in a more contemplative life of teaching or lecturing or writing or counseling.

Doing is his métier. His tremendous ability, energy, and unique experience will continue to be applied in public service.

3/15/64

It's hard to put your finger on just what it was about Dwight Eisenhower that gave him his unique place in the hearts of his countrymen.

War hero? Not really. He never personally led a charge up any San Juan hills, nor did he Dewey any enemy fleets at Manila Bay.

A spectacular, dramatic, colorful President and Presidency? No one would so describe the Eisenhower years.

Smile and charisma? Many an actor, legitimate and/or political, has exuded more Instant Charm.

No, it wasn't any of the obvious pedestal things. It wasn't his Greatness with a capital G; rather it was his goodness— without a capital G; the compelling decency of the man; the unconscious yet visible guidance by his conscience.

My own exposures to Ike were limited but, understandably, treasured.

Along with a couple of million other young men, I worked under him in World War II as a section sergeant in a machine gun platoon. I didn't share in his decision making, but had no complaints or reservations in assisting to carry out his conclusions.

My first real personal exposure came at a half hour meeting with him at SHAPE in March 1951. I flew the Atlantic in a two-decker Boeing Clipper bearing 10,000 signatures urging him to be a presidential candidate. He had refrained from discussing politics at SHAPE, but the key men then urging him to run figured that he should know how the young—I was one then—felt about the country's need of him.

He accepted the petition and quizzed me closely as to

how young Americans felt about their country's responsibility in the Free World. Taft, the Republican front runner, was considered basically isolationist, and it worried Ike that a President thus inclined might jeopardize the UN as well as NATO. His manner was grave, and he was obviously perplexed as to just what his responsibility was to prevent that from happening. Could he? Should he?

After our discussion he took me out to join other dignitaries gathered for the formal welcome of Greece and Turkey into NATO. There was a playing of anthems, a raising of the Turkish and Greek flags, and a general exchange of amenities. Pretty impressive stuff for a former staff sergeant.

Politicking as such was never to his liking, but he extended aid and comfort when I carried the Republican gubernatorial banner in New Jersey with an impressive lack of success in 1957. After my thumping he wrote: "I am sorry that things did not work out as we had hoped for you, but I appreciate greatly your taking your defeat as only one round of the battle. This year has not been a particularly good one, in any respect, but I hope that 1958 will mean to our Party and to America a better and brighter year."

Ike wasn't Great.

He was great.

4/15/69

In the early years of his prominence, I tended to view Senator Everett Dirksen as a mellifluous anachronism. At times I thought all he needed was a string tie and white cloth vest to be a reincarnation of some of those storied old senatorial windbags.

As time went on, however, I developed a genuine regard for this unique American politico. As a Dewey and Ike supporter, I discovered, as they did, that behind his dulcet voice and gentle, shaggy bearing was firm conviction and great political sagacity. Quite often I found myself, as a fellow Republican, disagreeing with the causes he championed. He roused both my ire and respect, not because of his opposing view but because his relentless advocacy was so often successful.

With both his words and his political knowhow, he, more than any single man—including the President—is responsible for the passage of the civil rights measure. It is a nettle he grasped; from it in his own constituency he doubtless will get more headache and heartache than applause.

In pouring his labor, his accumulated wisdom, his all into this vital struggle, he lifted himself from the political category of prominence to the vastly less populated category of greatness.

7/15/61

Have you not sometimes said, "Now, if I could name the candidate, I'd pick . . ."?

The man I'd name isn't a candidate, hasn't even been mentioned as a possibility, and is about as likely to be nominated as you or I.

Yet his name is better known than most of those talked about. Better known because he has often and so well served in public office. He has been a candidate for the nomination. Not once. Not twice. But three times. He was *twice* the Republican standard bearer.

Right.

Thomas E. Dewey.

It's funny, isn't it, how quickly fame fleets in the presidential prospects' stable. It was, believe it or not, almost twenty years ago that Governor Dewey was elected President during the summer and up to and including the early edition of the *Chicago Tribune*. His term terminated late in the evening of the actual election day, November 2, 1948.

Governor Dewey was a man of extraordinary ability as a leader, as an administrator, as a politician, as a get-things-doner. His presidential platforms as well as his gubernatorial performance reflected both sense and social conscience. The programs he blueprinted and the ones he carried out reflected in the soundest way real concern for the public weal as well as encouragement for private enterprise. As the country's most important governor he was neither soupy nor sappy. He was forthright, tough, and sensibly imaginative.

Today, two decades later, Governor Dewey is a man of extraordinary ability as a leader, as an administrator, as a politician, as a get-things-doner.

All the other enumerated virtues are still there.

Plus the very appealing qualities of mellowness, warmth, twinkle, that sometimes in the long ago of the forties weren't evident.

Governor Dewey would have been quite a President when he first sought the nod in 1940 and was run over in the convention by the Willkie stampede.

Governor Dewey would have been an able President had he been elected in 1944, when the American people decided not to do a Midstream Swap.

Governor Dewey would have been a great President when he came within an eyelash of being elected in 1948.

Governor Dewey would be a great President in 1968, although he is not about to seek or get the job.

9/1/67

Most standard among the fulsome phrases always used by politicians while introducing, nominating, saluting, and salutating one another is the phrase "Great American."

But there really are some, and a truly Great among them is David Lawrence. One of this veteran journalistic gentleman's extraordinary accomplishments is *U.S. News & World Report*, which weekly keeps the Informed informed with lively and comprehensive editorial vitality.

During much of my father's lifetime David Lawrence's lucid commentary enlightened and influenced the country, and he has continued to do so to this day.

Often on one specific issue or another you and I might differ with his view, but for four decades everyone directing or concerned with events of our time has benefited from his being and saying.

I was reminded of this by something that appeared last June in "Tomorrow," a regular feature of *U.S. News & World Report*:

Nor does the notion sit well that U.S. has passed its glory, is *collapsing as a power* on the world stage. *Critics* overlook many dynamic sources of real and lasting U.S. strength. No nation comes close to *industrial might* of U.S., its remarkable farm productivity, its technical know-how. *Output* of this nation still is equal to *combined* total of next four leaders: Russia, Japan, West Germany and France.

Visitors find *other sources of vitality*. Europe, as they describe it, is complacent, ignores big-city problems of congestion, crime, pollution.

U.S. is unhappy about all these things, is struggling to cure its ills.

Then look ahead: Population of the country is growing younger, better-educated, less provincial. Too: America, promising *newcomers* a share in the highest personal income of any nation in history, attracts more immigrants than any other place on earth. *That's another source* of future vitality.

Troubles in U.S.? Sure. *But it's a mistake to get carried away by gloom.*

David Lawrence didn't write that.

Perhaps much more important, he inspired and published it.

11/15/71

Papa Doc Duvalier, Haitian dictator, who for the past dozen years has ruled voodoo-ridden Haiti by means of pistol-packing hoods and hooligans, is now giving thought to his mortality. According to Benjamin Welles, the deceasing of Immortals Nasser and de Gaulle has made the Doctor think of his future, or rather, the lack of it.

I will never forget my first and only visit to Port-au-Prince, capital of this povertied paradise, aboard a private boat. Castro was then roaming the Cuban hills, picking up popular support to overthrow Batista. Neighboring governments were as nervous as the one in Havana.

On docking, an unlikely looking roughneck with a full-of-bullets belt and pistol sauntered aboard and genially asked if we would like to visit President Duvalier. It seems Duvalier had seen us sail in and decided to say hello.

The visit itself was storybook stuff. We were driven to the palace, whose grounds and corridors were loaded with lounging, disheveled riflemen, and waited in the Louis XIV ballroom for a bit before being escorted into the President's office. There he sat, smiling pleasantly. He'd not been President long, and it was expected that as a practitioner of medicine he would strive to up the health and living standards of his heavily populated, small country. He gave sensible answers, and he outlined his needs.

But there was more than a hint of both his plans for rule

and his reflection of fear: One pile of papers on his desk was held down by a pistol, and the other by a box of bullets.

Now, more than a dozen years later, this ruthless and bloodied boss thinks of his mortality, and so do his countrymen. With hope.

What wasted opportunity.

What a way to go.

2/15/71

Isn't it astonishing and wasn't it almost totally unforeseen that the sudden, total political demise of de Gaulle would have so little impact on the affairs of men and nations as to be considered really no impact at all?

Only two weeks after de Gaulle handed himself his head and went walking on Eire, I visited very briefly in France and Italy and Germany, and, do you know, only once did anyone bring up the name or the subject of his own accord.

This, mind you, just a dozen days after the long-predicted deluge. At least if the man had died, people would have been talking about his funeral and his life. Instead, alive, he has passed into oblivion. He will probably only once again be front-page news—and that won't be in his lifetime.

The referendum over which President de Gaulle immolated himself should and quite possibly would have been approved on its merits. By making himself the issue instead of leaving the issue itself as the issue, he killed both.

I am sure that for the man himself the greatest tragedy is that at his end there wasn't one.

7/1/69

Kudos and Brickbats

You and I may think we have a thing or two to do, decisions to make, responsibilities. But can you even imagine managing a private enterprise whose assets are bigger than those of General Motors, Standard Oil of New Jersey, U.S. Steel, and IBM all put together; an outfit daily dealing with multimillions of customers whose each transaction averages only dimes or so, each of whom gets billed monthly with items running into the dozens; an outfit that yearly needs to raise $8.5 billion in cash for new plant and equipment; an outfit that has to cope with regulatory agencies in fifty states and more on the federal level?

To run at all a business so incomprehensibly huge would seem well nigh impossible—yet American Tel. & Tel., despite an occasional rash of wrong numbers, *is* run and extraordinarily well run.

Looking at theirs, we might even find comfort in the relative proportions of our own problems. I'm glad AT&T's in Mr. de Butts' hands rather than in yours or mine.

6/1/72

There is no surer guarantee of business success than giving customers their money's worth—or a bit more. Many merchants and manufacturers find doing this profitably very difficult.

Do you know of anyone who has done it more successfully, in a most competitive field, than Sears and J. C. Penney?

It isn't all that often one can walk into a store and know with such a high degree of certainty that most everything one buys there will be as low or lower in price and high or higher in quality than anywhere else. At Sears and J. C. Penney this is invariably so.

The result?

Success. Big success.

6/1/69

It's fun to be right at least once in a while. Here six months ago, I wrote: "The A & P, once enormously successful and still the largest chain of food stores, has responded to tough competition and ever thinner profit margins by setting out on a suicidal spree of price cutting. . . . The whole thing is one of the most incomprehensible major industry capers in the annals of American business."

With an $800 million sales increase last year, A & P's WEO-CEO geniuses managed to rack up a $51 million loss.

6/1/73

These multi-multibillion dollar "deals" with Russia are largely hot air because they involve a lot of hard cash of which Russia hasn't got that much and the United States isn't about to supply in those telephone-number quantities.

Dr. Hammer is unquestionably a big operator, but press releases won't produce the capital needed to lubricate even barter agreements of that announced magnitude.

So, forget the talk of billions in United States–Soviet trade relations. They reflect a desire, not reality.

That the desire is there is all to the good—and about all and the only good that will emerge for a long time.

5/15/73

The season's over, the ski season, that is. At least for the Head skier.

Learning that Howard Head had melted all but 1 percent of his holdings in the company that bears his name, *Forbes* was curious as to why.

Ski's Head wasn't talking.

But his P.R. man knows *his* way down a slippery slope. His explanation: By selling the stock, Mr. Head hoped that more Head stock on the open market would aid Head in its mergers, acquisitions, and other expansion plans.

How's that for a snow job?

5/1/70

RCA's Robert Sarnoff should be enjoying some of the enjoyment his corporation's earnings should be providing shareholders. One of these days, enough investors are going to realize how inadequately RCA's present P/E ratio reflects its value.

8/1/73

In Denver not long ago a friend told me that somebody told him that Moshe Dayan had attributed much of Israeli military success to the fact that "We put doctors and lawyers up front—they know how to charge."

12/1/73

The company which makes the most money from do-it-your-self homework is Band-Aided Johnson & Johnson.

8/1/73

Ask any businessman to name instantly half a dozen good-guy corporations and I'll bet Xerox and Coca-Cola will be mentioned most often. There are multiple Reasons Why, of course. Two more have come to recent attention. Xerox's Peter McColough (who has a tough act to follow when it comes to broad-gauge business thinking as displayed by his predecessor, Joseph Wilson) has announced that annually twenty or so employees will be given a year's leave of absence at full pay and with all benefits to work in a social-service out-fit of their own choice, whether it be concerned with drug addicts, mine safety, civil rights, or what have you—so long as the activity is free from partisan politics and profit-making, and is legal.

The other example comes from Coca-Cola's comprehensive Heart-felt but Head-using program for the thousand or so who labor at harvesting in Minute Maid's orange groves. A recent editorial calling attention to the often shocking conditions of crop-picking workers brought a lot of letters defending or accusing. As usual, Coke is providing answers instead of parrying questions.

Whoever still thinks corporate profits preclude expenses for meeting social problems should look at these two outfits, because now—and every year more so—it becomes clear that you can no longer have the former without the latter.

10/1/71

According to one of *The Wall Street Journal*'s absorbing feature articles, "American Express is again left holding the bag" in what appears to be another bizarre fraud—though this time the scale is vastly less than in the Salad-Oil-That-Wasn't instance.

Maybe American Express ought to insist that those to whom they are going to extend credit should show a Bank-Americard for identification.

5/1/71

LOEW'S
Reaching new ones all the time.

5/15/70

A corporate giant, despite muscle and prowess, can discover that success is no guarantee against an occasional flooring by a nimble newcomer.

Take Eastman Kodak. Huge. Capable. Research-minded. Marketing master. Ably directed. Dominant for decades in its field, not only because of sheer size but also as a result of constant attention to developing tomorrow's products while today's are still successful sellers.

Yet look at two developments absolutely up its alley which Eastman Kodak almost totally missed—two misses which others have turned into truly great successes.

Office copiers.

Ironically enough, the greatest in this new industry, Xerox, turned Kodak's Rochester in seven years from a one-company town into a two-company town.

And Polaroid. Instant picture making, including instant color.

Anytime any tycoon thinks his company knows all the answers and is here to stay disirregardless, he need only think a bit about the foregoing.

Eastman Kodak is pretty much as good as they come, has rarely taken its formidable accomplishments for granted, has never long been complacent, but even it doesn't have omniscience and all the answers all the time.

In today's garrets are many of tomorrow's corporate giants.

4/1/67

A letter to shareholders from Crocker National Corporation, the California-headquartered bank holding company, opens with this paragraph: "Crocker National Corporation earnings increased in each quarter during 1972. However, the gains were not sufficient to bring the corporation's earnings for the full year to 1971 levels."

One of their shareholders sent it to us with the comment, "How's that now?"

If I were a Crocker depositor, I'd sure as heck check my monthly statements with considerable care—if the foregoing is an example of their addition!

5/1/73

It's always a disappointment when we witness a Good and Godly Corporation hit the low road after decades on the high one.

In the quality and ingenuity of its products; in its treatment of employees, distributors, and customers; in its public relations and advertising, Caterpillar for years has always been an outstanding example of enlightened self-interest.

Their current advertising—blatant car-accident scare stuff—lobbies all out for making secondary roads wider, straighter, flatter, as if road spending didn't have a sufficient hunk of present government revenues, as if there were not other crying needs needing a tiny fraction of the money being spent on highways.

I guess Caterpillar has accustomed us to expecting a broader view from them than this crude self-serving.

5/1/72

When a fissure off the California coast started pumping and dumping oil on the nearby towns and beaches, everybody started jumping on Union Oil. Matters weren't helped one iota by a manufactured "quotation" attributed to Union's president, Fred Hartley, alleging his amazement at the publicity "for the loss of a few birds."

The situation is really ironic. Union Oil is one of the more ably managed giants in the business, and its service stations are notable for cleanliness and service.

Fred Hartley never said what the press reported, as the transcript and the Senate committee members definitely established. But I don't suppose the truth will ever catch up with the more colorful falsehood.

That means must be devised to head off such disasters in the future is without question. But any of the oil companies operating offshore could have been operating the rig where this first-of-its-kind accident occurred.

If villains are called for, obviously a huge number can be located, including—as he was the first to say—former Secretary of the Interior Stewart Udall, who granted the drilling rights and who has been one of the most successful conservationists who ever headed the department.

To heap all the blame on Hartley and Union is utter nonsense, and the fair-minded should help in offsetting what-

ever damage the narrow-minded may be doing to a first-rate
company.

3/15/69

Now the takeoverers are trying to bag the banks.

Leasco, a computer-leasing outfit that didn't exist four
years ago and can exist today only through the indulgent
sufferance of size-wary IBM and other computer manufacturers, reportedly is after one of New York's outstanding
banks—the Chemical, founded in 1823, and which now has
about $9 billion in assets.

Until he died, my father was a Chemical Bank enthusiast and customer; to a degree, we still are. But the day
takeoverers, be they ever so nimble, take over any bank we do
business with, we won't anymore.

Can you imagine entrusting your banking needs and
your trust in banks to The Operators?

If the existing regulatory agencies that are supposed to
protect depositors and supervise the fiduciary responsibilities
of the fiducists cannot prevent this sort of vault assault, then
I'll wager there's action to enact some new act by the Feds.
Which will probably go too far.

3/1/69

One of these days—

Gulf Oil will find a replacement for Bill Whiteford.
I hope.

4/15/73

Rolls-Royce is broke—unless Parliament in effect takes it on.
It won a huge aircraft engine contract in competitive bidding
against United Aircraft and General Electric by contracting

to deliver something, it turns out, that it could not at anything like the promised price.

There are cries in Britain that their government should bail the company out and lots of pleas that our government should help.

In heaven's name, why?

A business that gets business by landing orders by bidding below cost doesn't long stay in business. That's what free enterprise is all about.

Douglas Aircraft Company was in trouble a while ago. McDonnell took them on, and the combination under that tough, able pioneer, James McDonnell, has resulted in a strong and successful company. The same should be allowed or encouraged to happen to Lockheed. In near-total trouble on its own, Lockheed is further crippled by Rolls-Royce's failure. There's talk that our government should bail them out, keep them alive.

Why? We still have a number of huge and able defense-oriented companies in business. What's viable of Lockheed might be taken over by one or another of them. If all these companies cannot survive as is, attrition will determine the survivors.

For our government to keep alive every defense-oriented corporation—or *any* giant corporation—is impossible, undesirable, unnecessary, and would be an unmitigated wrong.

We have what is still essentially a free enterprise system.

Companies are free to make money in a competitive climate.

Free to be as enterprising as they can.

Free to make mistakes.

And free to go broke.

If the Food and Drug Administration goes after unprescribed patent medicines as they say they are, American Home Products may need some of its own nostrums.

4/1/72

For quite long now, corporations—especially the big ones—have been undergoing multiple assaults for matters that didn't used to be considered germane to running a successful business.

• From civil righters seeking business underwriting and more jobs for minorities from top rank to rank and file.

• From consumer groups, spurring and spurred by regulatory agencies.

• From ecologists more concerned with the preservation of wilderness than jobs.

• From aroused antipollutionists, pressing sometimes for too swift, unaffordable, and unavailable solutions.

• From the naïve and well-meaning seeking "democracy" on boards of directors.

• From the Naders to the nadirists and the opportunists.

From all these have come accusations and propositions of a volume and vehemence quite new to top management.

Goaded by the merit of some of the criticism, too many Americans are finding themselves in the ranks of armies led by extremists.

Now is a good time to weigh these words of James Roche, a prime target while chairman of General Motors: "Profits are the incentive, the driving force, behind economic expansion and rising employment. It takes almost $25,000 of investment to create one new job opportunity. Just to keep pace with our rising labor force in the year ahead will require that we open up 1.75 million new jobs."

In being mindful of other worthwhile corporate objectives, we'd better not lose sight of the primary objective of business—*staying* in business.

No profits, no business.

9/1/72

Oh, say, can't Meany see—

What Samuel Gompers so clearly saw at organized labor's early dawn (and I quote)—"The worst crime against working people is a company that fails to make a profit."

5/15/72

The other day the head men of the railway workers unions solemnly announced that they want the government to own and run the nation's railroads. This reverses what had been their policy for forty-five years.

The reasons are so transparent as to be amusing.

In previous decades these unions "defended" private railway ownership because, with government encouragement, they were able to push management and stockholders all over their railway yards. The word *featherbedding* became a synonym for contract settlements satisfactory to the rail unions.

When the inevitable happened and railroad after railroad lumbered into bankruptcy, there came a slow, painful awakening: Featherbedding was no longer affordable if the railroads were to resume solvency, if they were to compete successfully with the highways, airways, and waterways.

Now that study after study, commission after commission, court after court has rules against the more flagrant abuses; now that managements are fighting back with an energy born of desperation; now that regulatory agencies show a commonsense interest in railway survival by consolidation instead of pushing for their extinction by pettifogging harassment—*now* the unions want the government to take over the railroads.

If one were given to the slightest cynicism, one might think the unions favor this course because of their long-proven power to push politicos around, to have them do their bidding. Since the privately owned railroads no longer have the dollars and cents to meet senseless demands, the unions figure the federal treasury will make a better trough.

Thank goodness the Johnson Administration is hardly likely to take this demand very seriously.

2/15/65

It's not just cynics who suspect that the unions involved not only wouldn't mind if the railroads went broke, but would likely be pleased at that result.

Why?

On the premise that the bankrupt railroads would then have to be nationalized. With the government owning both the railroads and the Treasury, and with the unions' political clout, labor figures the pickings should be easier, and ever bigger, ever better.

Nice prospect, eh?

2/1/73

Grant Simmons, Jr., fourth-generation head of the famed bedding firm, was asked how Simmons reacted to the water bed craze.

"We didn't. A water bed is the worst of both worlds. You can't sleep on it for the motion, and love on one is only possible for those young enough to perform in midair.

"In fact, these days you can only find water beds in those shops featuring beads and bongo drums."

10/15/72

United States Customs is a $2-billion-a-year business with 9,300 civil service workers sharing multiple and complicated responsibilities under United States laws.

For Americans returning from foreign travels and for foreigners visiting America, this important arm of the U.S. Treasury Department boils down to the neatly uniformed man who checks out one's bags and boxes to see that what isn't allowed in isn't brought in, and that duty for what's dutiable over the $100 allowance is collected. These inspectors have a job of unique difficulty, unique importance.

For the tired, usually glad-to-be-back American tourist, this short session with the Customs man is the first contact on the home front. For the foreigner, it is his first real contact with Americans in fabulous, fabled America. The Customs inspector is supposed to achieve two, sometimes incompatible, things: Convey a cheerful, polite welcome while rummaging through one's luggage to be sure that the relevant laws of this land are not being violated—intentionally or unintentionally.

Try that job out sometime. For eight hours at a clip. Going through hundreds of assorted suitcases and all manner of containers full of dirty laundry, new antiques, grotesque souvenirs. Luggage belonging to fat, sweaty, pushing, belligerent people; to thin, cold people; to people who may or may not speak English, sometimes printable, sometimes not; mothers with squawling children; to big men and to bad men.

To coin a phrase, I should think the task would drive a saint nuts, and frankly I marvel at the equanimity and the genuine helpfulness with which these fellows get 99 plus 44/100 percent of their job done.

This was all brought to mind when I read in the papers recently several letters chewing out the U.S. Bureau of Customs.

As one who has to travel often into and out of many countries, I've been through countless other Customs. I don't recall ever seeing tourists in any land have any difficulties. With returning native sons, however, it's frequently a far different story.

If any returning American thinks he gets much of an examination, he ought to watch British Customs give returning Englishmen a going over! I have seen their inspectors take Britons returning from a weekend abroad and turn their luggage literally almost inside out—and make them do likewise with all their suit pockets and the coats over their arms.

Through Kennedy alone over 2 million come pouring past the Customs man.

Out of these tens of thousands perhaps two dozen are loud or nasty in their beefs. On behalf of the other thousands of us, who have some appreciation for what is done and how well it is done by our Customs men, a salute and warm "thank you" is long past due.

In all fairness—could any of us handle this tough job half as well, if at all?

8/15/65

Mostly the U.S. Department of Agriculture is one of those cabinet-level outfits of which one hears little, and is most often headed by someone whose name nobody can quite recall.

But (z) things are different these days. They've had to make some really Big Decisions and have consistently come up with monumentally wrong answers.

The Ruskies take our U.S. Aggies on both price and quantity in wheat deals—the Agriculture Department was so unaware of the size of the Russian and world wheat shortage that officials first bragged about disposing of hundreds of millions of bushels at a huge loss to the United States.

At the same time, for years they have been pounding on the State Department's door to get better export opportunities for such major American farm products as soybeans. Then, just when such exports can hugely help our balance-or-trade payments, they make a stupid—and soon modified—decision to embargo the export of such commodities in temporary short supply on the home front. This unthinking, arbitrary cutoff will set back our farm-export negotiations considerably more than any tariff discrimination.

What's with those Seers and Sayers in the Department of Agriculture who are sowing such seedy policies?

8/15/73

That butt of all the cartoonists, the butt of all the intellectuals advocating rampaging freedom, the butt of all the bewailers of privilege and profit is turning out to be the guy who most effectively is goring the theorists and the practitioners of communism. I'm referring to the aging, balding, fat old capitalist who works all day and most every day running his business profitably.

Our ivory towerists, who write with will and so well about the absolute necessity of freedom to think and to write and to do, have splintered their lances against communist dictatorships in vain, have for decades seen their verbal shafts valiantly but vainly shattered against the idiotologists of communism. They have been scorned when not ignored, ridiculed when not reviled by the gospelers of the Red dictatorships.

Lo and behold, in recent years the tremblings, the fissures in communist ranks and lands have been wrought by the efficient production achievements of the bloated, vested, cigar-smoking cartoon–tycoons. The Reds envy the knowhow and would emulate the achievements of our capitalists. Red leaders have learned the hard way that productivity can neither be built, can neither run nor start nor be started without that very small spark plug called incentive.

Thus the practice of capitalism and the virtue of profit are shaking, reducing the ranks of communists. They see that in fact communism costs not merely freedom but also the material productivity their system was *supposed* to stimulate.

James Reston, the clear-eyed oracle of *The New York Times*, put it more briefly and better in a dispatch from Moscow some months ago:

> It is interesting here that Communist officials, who used to believe that capitalist economic ideas would certainly fail, are now more afraid of Western economic theory than of Western political theory.
>
> Western Europe is being unified, not by the political philosophers, or the Western statesmen, but by the American scientists and businessmen with their computers and their capital. This is what is worrying officials in Moscow.
>
> 8/1/69

Communism is confusin' if not amusin'.

Those of us opposed to it seem more certain of what it is than those who embrace it. China, Russia, and Yugoslavia each warred over the Word as preached and practiced by the others.

"Monolithic" communism?

It would seem it has more deviations than India has dialects.

3/15/72

In these striking times there's an understandable tendency on the part of those struck to deplore with vehemence the ready availability of unemployment compensation for workers not working.

In fact, only a fraction of those collecting unemployment compensation are strikers. And, despite innumerable stories by innumerable businessmen, only a small percentage of those collecting unemployment compensation are unwilling to work.

In these times of wide and widening unemployment—reaching near to 5 million at the moment—it shouldn't take much thought or long reflection to make one glad, not mad, that unemployment compensation is as substantial as it is and of as long duration as it is.

If it were not for the sizable underpinning that such compensation is today providing to the economy, this recession would have been on its way to becoming a real depression.

There are few businesses throughout the country that have not reduced payroll numbers in these tightened times. A principal reason that such action hasn't snowballed the downslide is unemployment compensation.

Don't knock it.

Be glad of it.

1/1/71

The disastrous impact of lengthy unemployment of family breadwinners needs no documentation. As in the case of the other fellow's toothache, it is easy to extend one's sympathy without feeling the pain.

Rightly, most attention and most attempts to tackle unemployment emphasize the dire situation confronting a workless man with a family to support. His problems are immediate and imperative.

Less pressing, but perhaps wreaking greater individual havoc, is unemployment of the quite young—the teen-agers out of school or no longer able to afford school. For youth, with a vitality unvitiated by age, drift often means disaster.

The young have to be doing, and if it cannot be the doing of work, it is sometimes the doing of bad. A man of more years, and particularly a man with a family, has the maturity of experience. He doesn't seek to solve his galling idleness with what the psychologists call antisocial activities. It is established that among the 4.7 million unemployed, 709,000 are under twenty years of age. Before these young people have the habit of work, they have had to learn to cope with idleness, to develop a busy life doing nothing. Sourness and cynicism are the inevitable accompaniments.

2/15/63

Energy and Ecology

Until we're stunned into action-producing awareness of our snowballing energy crisis by some Pearl Harbor-type catastrophe or Sputnik-like spur, we the people, I guess, will simply continue the present drift to the brink of an energy disaster.

The present and continuing standoff between well-motivated, oft-misguided and misinformed environmentalists and those who need and those who have to provide energy is quite apt, you know, to result with both winning their points at the price of losing what has to be and *is* essentially the same objective.

Believe me, when businesses all over the land have their energy rationed and job hours reduced, when homes have only certain hours that their lights can light, their hot water run hot, and their ice boxes run cold, I think it will make re-election a bit difficult for the senator or the congressman or the mayor or the governor or the state legislator who resolutely blocked every attempt at intelligent cooperation in developing additional power resources, be they atomic or coal or other.

Additional power is achievable without excluding, precluding, or even occluding ecologists—but not in the present emotional climate, a climate that results, of course, in major part from decades of waste and wantonness and unawareness on the part of energy users and suppliers.

If I were President—and I guess it's among a few million other reasons why I'm not—within the next year or two I would awaken the public to the growing direness of our energy shortage and thus provide the impetus toward solution and resolution, by announcing the forthcoming inauguration of gasoline rationing à la World War II. *Then* we would find a swift drive for an intelligent solution, compromise, balance between rain-wetted fields and irrigated ones.

12/1/72

Maybe we should get smart like some of these international wheeler-dealers. Since there's just no way the Saudi Arabians can buy enough air-conditioned Cadillacs to use up the tens of billions of dollars that they will be getting for their oil, and since there's little likelihood that Libya's Colonel can get rid of all his tens of billions of additional oil revenues by continuing to finance revolutions and revolutionaries (because the revolutionaries will all have so much money they'll want to enjoy it a bit), we should encourage these Arabian Aladdin-oil-lamp lands to invest their money in American businesses at an ever faster pace.

Then when they become majority owners of, say, Standard Oil and General Motors and IBM and the like, we can get very emotionally excited about all them f'reigners "owning" the United States, and "nationalize" Standard Oil and General Motors and IBM.

Sort of have our cake—er, energy—and eat it too.

You think that's a joke, son?

12/1/72

We're at war—bloodless, thank God.

The energy crisis should and soon will have an impact on this nation not unlike that of World War II. If we attempt to guns-and-butter our way through it, it'll simply compound the damage to the people, our country, our character, our worth in every sense of the word.

I think most Americans are far readier to meet the crisis than the politicians are to recognize we have one.

Immediate short-term steps—50 mph, lowered thermostats, turning lights out, daylight-saving time year-round —will reduce the up-to-now soaring rate of increase in energy consumption in this country. They will do little to relieve what will soon be a quantitive *decrease* in the energy heretofore available.

Gasoline rationing is a must, and the sooner the better—

if the number of factories closed and workweeks (and pay packets) shortened, and curtailed school and office hours and days, are to be less than now seems likely. Given the choice, man would opt to drive his car less than to work less and take home less. The sooner he understands that the choice is clear and unequivocal, the greater the possibility he'll not have to undergo both. A sure way for President Nixon to renew his Gallup is to do the unpopular but needful: to impose gasoline rationing not as a last resort but a first essential.

The impact of all this on the economy shouldn't be hard to project, but for many it seems to be. I think this energy crisis has to end up being almost all good for all of us, for our country, its future and ours.

Sure, it'll play hobs with Detroit for a while; be disruptive to the economy while emphasis and demand shuffle and shift. There's even a possibility that, if the impact is as impactful as it now seems sure to be, inflation could be tempered a while by hesitant consumers.

Not for long, though.

As a result of sharp curtailment of gasoline consumption, by spring there will be enough fuel for schools, factories, the petrochemical industry, etc., to meet nearly all productive needs.

And when you're working as much as ever at prevailing or better wages, the money you can't spend for gasoline and have saved by saving on home heating and light bills and from the postponed purchase of a new car or the difference in price between the little one and the big one you might have once bought, and the money saved by not driving on your vacation—all will combine to enable you to buy the storm windows, the extra blankets, sweaters, fireplace wood, and the thousand and one other things that we all buy when we have an extra buck.

Spending patterns will be redirected, not curtailed.

Travel? The lure of going abroad will be better 'n ever because the buck will once again—and soon—be the highly desirable commodity it used to be in foreign lands. It wasn't merely the $80-billion surplus of greenies sloshing around the world that devalued, demeaned the dollar. Even more, it was the indisputable geometric arithmetic of the money that we were spending and would be continuing to spend on oil from other lands—an estimated additional $50 billion *annually* in a few years—that no amount of soybean sales could have paid for. Our trade deficit seemed inevitable and inexorable because we were unwilling to exercise any retraint in our zooming, substantially wasteful consumption of energy.

Now all that is being precipitously ended.

We Americans are not really as compulsively wasteful or helplessly indulgent as some in the world have come to believe. Challenged, we respond.

Challenged we are.

And respond we will.

12/1/73

If the Big Oils' Big Men don't look further down the road right *now*, they're vastly dumber than they're paid to be.

No one really expects 'em to fund an all-out research program on, say, solar energy—but, controlling perhaps as much as one-third of the United States' privately owned coal reserves, couldn't they get cranked up now on a crash basis to finding the most economic ways and means of turning that stuff into an affordable energy? I get the impression that mostly they're sitting down and beefing because Congress doesn't appropriate more money to do that job.

If the Big Oils think their primary "public relations" mission in life these days is to tell Americans to drive less

and less fast, do they really think they are making much contribution either to their future or to ours?

If their thinking continues to run in this direction, it's
time to bail out of oil stocks because the Qaddafis of Where-
The-Oil-Is ain't gonna keep 'em in business on their present
scale.

Maybe our Big Oil Chiefs *are* knee deep and $ multi-
millions deep in exploring any and every feasible supplement
to oil. If so, it's an unbelievably well-kept secret.

We're not talking about a substitute for oil.

We're talking about supplements to oil.

If our private giants insist that it's principally the government's business to find all the answers, then what alternative do we and the government have but to make Energy
the public's public business?

10/1/73

OUR ENERGY PROBLEMS
are too important to be left to the Oilheads.

12/1/73

Over the veritably unanimous disapproval of the rest of the
Forbes Investment Committee on the company's Thrift Plan
and Retirement Plan, I exercised a rarely exercised preroga-
tive of sole stockholder and requested the sale of our long-
held Exxon shares.

Why?

Two reasons: first, to put both our Funds more substantially in cash, a rather useful commodity in the event
of a predepression recession of alarming proportions. I don't
say it will happen—but I don't say it won't, either.

Second, I don't think, despite all that's been written on

the subject of the present and further confiscation-with-remu-
neration-from-future-profits of the International Oils' international oil holdings, that enough has been made of the fact
that these International Oils are also going to have their re-
fineries and distribution networks in most countries of any
size either nationalized or veritably duplicated—harbor facilities, pipelines, stations, trucks, tankers: the works, the whole
works.

Take the French, just as a for-instance. How do you
think they like discovering that their special, superfriendly
"relationship" with the Arabs means damn little in saving
them from the oil shortage, because most of what they get
has to come through Rotterdam and International Oils' distribution and transportation system? So, too, Italy, England,
and all the others.

Knock their foreign-distribution systems out of earnings, and what does that do to the oil giants?

Now, beyond any shadow of a doubt, Exxon is the best-
managed of 'em all. And with all the cash from its confis-
cated/nationalized properties, it will be an even huger bank
than it now is. Further, its present management has its head
less stuck in an oil well than the others. Exxon *does* have at
least a toe in researching the practical development of other
energy sources. It will have the funds and doubtless be the
first to put a whole foot there soon.

Judging from the past, the others will continue to hold
coal, cry for its quickie use by strip-mining without greening,
and press for the opening of offshore and federal lands to new
drilling.

New drilling is needed and should come quickly, but it's
to the sun and in new ways of getting out coal and depollut-
ing the stuff that the broad energy future lies.

Exxon's more apt to see the light and to create the new

energy sources to keep alight than its brethren. If they dust off their foresight, I'll probably be sorry we sold our shares.

And that sorrow would make me very happy.

1/15/74

If those in Washington and elsewhere charged with making decisions on getting the oil out of Alaska have been putting their minds to the problem, it's high time they made them up. How many years does it take to determine what will be the least damaging and most efficacious way to make the black gold available?

With Sadat saber-rattling and reminding the United States in particular that the Arab world controls some 70 percent of the Free World's known oil reserves, we should stop this endless, costly horsing around.

Even if there is a slight ruffling of the ecology, an occasional annoyance to a tufted titmouse or two, I'm afraid the strength and security of free human beings should be given a priority.

3/1/72

The Federal Power Commission may not be the dumbest regulatory body in Washington, but its actions and lack of action on natural gas prices certainly make it seem that way.

Long before natural gas shortages zoomed, they loomed.

Now there's supposed to be nearly no end of the stuff somewhere in the ground. But, as with oil, it takes money for drilling to find it.

Even before the ecology prairie fire swept the nation, relatively unpolluting gas was in increasing demand for many compelling reasons, such as cleanliness and convenience. The power companies and the gas companies saw the shortage coming—yet the commission kept dragging its feet on rates that would make all-out new source searches profitable.

Now the economy and the ecology and the customers as well as the companies must suffer the *foreseen* shortages —and the FPC still hasn't moved effectively.

There are those who suspect the producers have dragged *their* feet to force higher prices, but I doubt if they are that collusively and criminally stupid. Anyway, the Federal Power Commission is checking out that unlikelihood.

But it's elementary, dear FPC, that when companies have customers piled up and coming out of their ears, they do their damnedest to meet demand because profit comes from selling at a reasonable profit what they've got to sell.

The fight against higher polluting by other energy sources and the soaring need for more energy have combined to create a severe squeeze. It would be far less severe if the commission had displayed a modicum of foresight.

Now it's even showing difficulty in displaying hindsight.

It's way past time the FPC got off its duff.

5/15/71

Rogers Morton, longtime sensibly liberal GOP politico and now Secretary of the Interior, recently told a congressional energy hearing that higher prices for natural gas would benefit consumers.

That statement is neither as silly nor as specious as it may first sound.

Natural gas, the least polluting major energy source, is in ever more demand and showing ever less domestic reserves. Despite the nearly insatiable market for gas, present prices are regulated so low that there is virtually no incentive for gas companies to engage in the expense of finding more within our borders.

Higher prices would certainly lessen demand, and close the present too-wide gap between the price of the domestic stuff and gas imported in liquefied form.

As Sherlock Holmes used to say to his sidekick, "Elementary, my dear Watson."

While on this subject: We *are* getting to the point where maybe people should be urged to use less rather than more. Changing the old ethic that growth and increased consumption are synonymous terms may prove difficult, but the ecology consciousness of so many so quickly would indicate that our values are as reevaluatable as our valuables.

5/1/72

I cannot think of a lone book which has had such a resounding impact on its subject matter as Rachel Carson's *Silent Spring* with its sweeping, frightening indictment of pesticides. The other day I asked my eight-year-old daughter to get me a can of bug spray so that I could de-mosquito the porch, where we were about to have supper. With a look of horror, she assured me that spraying the area would bring death not only to the bugs, but also the birds, the bees, the trees, and the people. Rather than be considered such a callous murderer in her eyes, I figured it was better to be bitten.

The eight-year-old set apparently is reflecting what they have heard from the parents of playmates, and the alarm has not been confined to porches and patios. It has reached Washington, and virtually overnight the chemical industry finds its $300 million pesticide divisions threatened with all manner of restriction.

I know nothing about the subject, but after reading Miss Carson's articles as they appeared in *The New Yorker*, an incident that had occurred three years ago came vividly back to mind. My wife and I were in Nassau and chanced to meet James Rand Jr., who for twenty-nine years ran Remington Rand. Mr. Rand, long a tough, brilliant tycoon, was then seventy-three and retired.

There was a basket of fruit nearby, and I offered him some. He asked if they had been washed. When I looked perplexed, he hastened to say that unwashed fruits, vegetables, and so forth could wreck one's health because of the widespread use of sprays and pesticides. "Even when washed, they may still be full of poison because of the chemicals that might have been put into the soil where they had been grown," he observed. I glanced at the liquid refreshment in his hand, smiled at him reassuringly, and tried to change the conversation. He seemed to sense that I wasn't taking him seriously and proceeded to whip out of his pocket a paperbound volume which he assured me would prove that we were all slowly being poisoned by pesticides.

I thought he was nuts at the time, and later remarked to my wife that it was a shame to see senility erode the mind of such a brilliant man. I never even glanced at the tract he had given me. But that was before Rachel Carson made even eight-year-olds aware of the situation.

8/15/63

The ending of major water pollution not only should be done—it *has* to be done. The foot laggers within an industry won't long maintain any cost advantage because, on local, state, and federal levels, prohibitions, penalties, and effective enforcement are all on the way.

While I ardently share the healthy American distaste for constantly widened federal regulation, some form of it is doubtless needed in this area. If *all* steel companies, for instance, are required to meet the same standard, presumably there would be no cost advantage by one over another. In some industries it could well be that a shortsighted, pigheaded management might refuse to spend the sum necessary to stop contamination and thus be able to sell for less than the good-citizen competitor.

Anyone who is now building a plant which normally includes processes that involve pollution is really negligent, nay, stupid if he doesn't build into it a method or means of meeting the problem. Converting older plants and processes will be more costly, but it must eventually be done.

No one runs a factory without figuring as a necessary operating expense the cost for power, the cost of heat, the cost of land, and so forth. From now on one must include the equally necessary cost of not polluting.

We have a great, big, rich, bountiful, bustling, growing, booming land, but it's not such a great, big, rich, bountiful, bustling, growing, booming land that we can get along without clear water.

Marie Antoinette may have thought cake could solve the bread shortage.

No one thinks gin can solve the water shortage.

11/15/65

Polluting the citizenry to death is poor business.

A long time ago *Forbes*' wee voice was raised along with others urging that industries join, industry by industry, to tackle the problem of fouling air and water.

It was probably unfeasible to expect voluntary cooperation on a project so costly, so vast, and so varied. Besides, if, say, the steel industry had joined in a joint effort, the government might have hopped all over them for violating some facet of the antitrust laws, or something.

Anyway, very properly if belatedly, the federal government is planning to move, under Johnsonian prodding, on a program to depollute the land. Only the Feds can operate across state borders, and since neither air nor water observes state and city boundaries, action on the Washington level seems essential.

The cost will be great for many a manufacturer, yet the cost of not spending this money threatens to be infinitely greater. Such expenditure must be considered as much a cost of running a plant as the cost of electricity and machinery and windows and workers. If all have to bear this expense, none should be overhurt competitively.

Ultimately, we who live long enough to survive present pollution will pay for it in the price of what we buy.

But what's wrong with that?

3/1/67

Thank heaven for Earth Day.

Imagine, youth aroused for something that even we parents, ever so obtuse and retarded as we may be, can applaud. While lengthening our lives here on earth may shorten our (heavenly) hereafter, a lot of us would make that sacrifice.

5/15/70

Antipollution is now as rampant in the land as pollution itself.

Fighting fouling the environment is a hotter campus cause nowadays than Vietnam, Chicago, college presidents, and *in loco parentis*.

Citizens write letters about sewerage emptying into rivers and sue to get results.

Many states and communities turn down new industries unless they can prove they're clean.

A national and international network of pollution-monitoring stations are under negotiation.

Universities are planning to grant degrees in ecology.

All but the youngest hot rodders are willing to give up some horses under the car hood if it means less poison in the air.

Will this massive outcry continue long enough to have effective results? Will federal and state laws be enacted with effective enforcement clauses? Will people be concerned long enough to pay the bill through higher prices? Will towns tolerate lost jobs when it proves too costly to "clean" obsolete plants? Will sensible subsidies be extended to enable the unfairly overburdened towns and companies and small businesses to do the necessary converting and treating?

I think so, but it sure won't be as easy as the present outcry and political oratory suggest.

The answers to preserving a livable environment are not all simple, and some of the nuts who are now pushing simplistic cure-alls won't help bring about any *lasting* solutions.

But this fabulous war is now well launched. It is in some ways indisputably the most valuable, worthwhile, and exciting war we in the world have ever waged. It's winnable, too, but as always with wars, there's a price.

But what is required in the way of things and design and construction and knowledge won't be poured into sterile weaponry. Meeting the needs of this war will indeed involve new billions of dollars, as well as the diversion of other billions from other programs.

And do you know the real kicker in the whole program?

In addition to being necessitous and good, the whole

effort to clean up so we can live is going to be *profitable* to those who provide ways and means, systems and cement, and pipe and chemicals, and just about every other thing you can think of.

There is not a thing wrong with Gain, and it's doubly exciting that it's for such completely gainful purposes.

P.S. Do you suppose everyone will get so aroused that fewer of us will continue throwing papers, wrappers, bottles, and cans onto city curbs and country roadsides? I suppose that would be asking too much.

4/1/70

MONSTERS—ENDANGERED SPECIES

A friend returning from Scotland reports that the fabled Loch Ness monster has really and finally died.

From pollution.

10/1/70

Fortunately, more and more people are getting alarmed about the ravages threatened by our pollution of all elements in our environment.

It really brings you up sharp when the Norwegian explorer Thor Heyerdahl says the most impressive thing about his recent papyrus boat drift across the Atlantic was that rarely were they ever out of sight of plastic debris and vast areas of oily muck.

Imagine, flotsam and jetsam strewn all across the great Atlantic. Depressing, isn't it?

10/1/69

The Nixon Administration has proposed that corporate expenditures for pollution control be permitted a rapid rate of write-off.

This would provide sensible incentive for something that must be done as soon, as rapidly, and as completely as possible.

It's one cost of doing business that the government should encourage to rise.

7/15/69

Depreciate pollution.

The cost of it, that is.

President Nixon's stepped up depreciation rate on business equipment provides an important stimulus for the economy. Modernization of machinery and equipment is a competitive must and has long been a source of our industrial strength at home and abroad.

The President or the Treasury Department should specifically include the same more rapid write-off for the enormous sums that so many businesses are now and must soon be spending for depollution. There is no longer an escape from that cost of living, but the cost of accomplishing it will not add anything to productivity.

The dollar value of enabling the customers to last a bit longer won't show up in the annual audit for a while.

Prompt promulgation of the necessary directives is very much in order.

2/1/71

Moved by vestiges of parental poundings on the virtues of thrift, I insist my wife buy bottles of pop and mix with screw tops whenever available so that what isn't drunk will keep its fizz till next time.

This directive recently ran smack up against an ultimatum from our concerned fifteen-year-old daughter, who demands the banishment of one-trip bottles on the basis that they add litterly to pollution. Unfortunately, it seems screw-top bottles come in no other except the No-Returns.

Now couldn't bottle makers put screw tops on returnable bottles of pop and keep us both happy?

11/15/70

Newest "in" color: tattletale gray.

Ever since ecology jumped out of the dictionary and hit the fan.

It's about time for some smart sheet, shirt, and under-garment maker to come out with all that stuff in this newest patriotic shade so that nobody who sees the housewife's freshly laundered laundry will think for a minute that she used any of that get-things-whiter stuff you're not supposed to use anymore.

The dirtier your laundry looks, the cleaner everything else is.

I guess.

12/1/71

If I were a maker of plastics and/or molder of plastic con-tainers and packaging, I'd put my R & D money to work evolving a plastic with some self-destruct capabilities.

With most people, and especially a sizable majority of young, now deeply and determinedly pollution-conscious, the makers who can say their stuff comes in containers that will dissolve or fade away in time under certain conditions will reap an immediate and immense market advantage. Surely, it's not beyond laboratory capability to develop a plastic that, say, after some weeks or months in salt water, will melt away.

A little imagination and a lot of research should result in a product with potential sales of unimaginable magnitude.

5/15/72

Garbage needn't necessarily remain just that.

Disposing of the stuff is a problem that seems to be increasing at a geometric rate. It presents a huge challenge to antipollution efforts; it costs a veritable mint to get rid of; and the areas for dumping it seem to diminish. Rats and racketeers—if you'll pardon the redundancy—abound in garbage. There is, though, a relatively simple and inexpensive way to make a plus out of our refuse minuses.

Squeeze 'em. Mash 'em. Make hunks of the whole mess.

It isn't hard to do. Machines from household- to city-size exist that can make "solid waste" out of the stuff we all throw out.

Stick a pin in nearly any part of the map of the United States and draw a circle with a ten-mile radius, and within it you'll find a dozen places that want or need or could benefit from being filled in. Millions monthly are paid to those trying to dispose of dirt and the like by those trying to fill in holes and other places. Compressed "bales" of garbage are easily transported and make ideal fill. A sprinkling of chemical antiseptic cologne, a covering of dirt, and presto! You have a uniquely well-fertilized transformation of the (w)hole to salable flat green.

This isn't as nonsensical as it sounds. Where the sorting necessary for recycling isn't feasible, by squaring the stuff you turn it into something useful.

In your own town or city, get 'em to start compressing and to sell the solid results. The bales may not be worth their weight in gold but, by golly, instead of costing money they'll produce revenue and do good.

A reversal of that old truth about waste and want.

2/15/72

Resolving Transportation Problems

"Government transport policy is like an octopus, with each arm assigned a different task. But no one hand knows what the others are doing. Not only that, one hand is frequently pulling and hauling against the others." Thus late last month spoke Daniel P. Loomis, president of the Association of American Railroads. It would be easy enough to write off Mr. Loomis' opinions as those of a man interested in having the government pull the railroad industry's rather badly singed chestnuts out of the fire. But today the railroads are not the only form of transportation that is in trouble. The commercial airlines are hardly better off. The decay of our commutation systems is threatening the life of the big cities. Trucks, barges, aircraft, and private autos are all jockeying for position in a situation where each operates under a different set of ground rules. In the case of the airlines and railroads, the situation is further complicated by the fact that each is under the control of a separate government agency. Each tends to be treated as a separate entity rather than as part of a single transportation industry.

Not only has the confusion produced a transportation system unworthy of the world's richest nation, but has actually undermined our capacity for national defense.

Railroads have special cause for complaint. Their regulation and taxation as we have it today dates back to a period when the railroads had a virtual monopoly of transportation. There was no national highway network, no airlines, little inland waterway traffic. Not only do the railroads continue to be shackled by restrictions put on them in their near-monopoly days, but the government virtually subsidized their rivals by building roads, airports, dredging rivers, and giving airmail subsidies.

Let's face it: Trucks, planes, barges, and buses are not really separate industries but part of a single vast transportation industry. Yet while airplanes and trucks operate on government-provided rights of way, the railroads must build and maintain their own—and pay taxes on them as well. Without specifically intending to do so, this setup penalizes one kind of transportation for the benefit of others.

What it all means is simply this: Until regulatory agencies begin to look at transportation overall rather than piecemeal, this country will never get the most transportation for the least money. The Transportation Act of 1958 did give Uncle Sam authority to deal with transportation as a whole. But not enough has been done to date. Development of a unified public policy of transportation must get high priority from the Administration that takes office next January.

10/1/60

President Eisenhower's proposal for a $50 billion highway modernization program has brought dramatically into focus one of our greatest needs. Most of us have become aware of the inadequacies of present highways through personal inconvenience during traffic-heavy days. But few realize the great cost of this delay and inconvenience—the cost to business of the delay in trucking shipments, the cost of death and hospitalization from resulting accidents, the waste of billions of gallons of gasoline from idling motors in traffic jams, etc.

It is to be hoped that, having outlined the need and suggested a course of action, the Eisenhower Administration will press to have the plan implemented.

8/1/54

Did you ever believe that you would live to see the day when someone in the position to say nay would actually say nay to those highway bulldozers that plow right through the hearts of cities and homes and people and landmarks?

Transportation Secretary John A. Volpe has done just that.

Highways that were throwing people out of homes are being held up until the thrown-out have a place to go. Highways are being detoured if the straight-line routing threatens obliteration of invaluable elements of heritage and environment.

Sure, we've got to have more highways.

But we've got to have places to live, and keep some places worth living in and on.

Vive le Volpe!

5/1/70

By a single switched vote, the Senate Public Works Committee decided to prohibit the use of any of the $5 billion in highway funds for urban transportation needs, such as subways and rapid rail systems.

With most of the nation's population living and working in the growing megalopolises, the asininity of continuing to sanctify gasoline tax revenues only for highways to and in cities that have no room for them has been recognized by the Nixon Administration.

With cities threatening to forbid private cars in choked streets, new modern mass transportation systems are a must.

A bill merely to allow states who want to use their part of federal transportation funds for such purposes failed to come out of committee when Vermont's Republican Senator Robert Stafford overnight switched his vote.

The reason he gave? "I come from a rural state, you know." And here all the time we thought he was a *United States* Senator.

Thus, thanks in major measure to Robert Stafford, more and more of Vermonters' growing federal income taxes will go to meet problems that could have been met from existing gasoline taxes.

10/1/72

One of these days someone in government is going to shake the bureaucratic dust from his mind and his feet, and/or someone in the aviation industry is going to think on a scale as big as the problem we face in connection with jetports.

Take New York, principal United States air getaway to and from the rest of the world. For a decade this great megalopolis has been bogged down on additional airport needs because those with the responsibility of solving the problem continue to think and act small, continue to view the need in the context of today's machines, next week's congestion, and in terms of getting jetports as close to urban heartlands as possible.

How blind can we be?

The airport of tomorrow, to serve the planes now blueprinted for tomorrow, should not, cannot, must not, and will not be located in urban-suburban heartlands. All well and good for existing, commuter-type airports, but simply *out* for the Giant Birds-to-be of continental and intercontinental dimensions.

In the area serving New Jersey, Philadelphia, as well as New York City, for instance, there's a huge flat sand-and-pine area near the Atlantic Ocean in New Jersey's Burlington County. Few homes, little industry, and not too many prospects of more. Will the Federal Aviation Agency, the Port of New York Authority, the State of New Jersey, or the State of New York *really* check it out?

No.

Why?

Because "it's too far away."

Too far away for whom?

It now takes anyone living in north Jersey who wants to fly to Europe about an hour and forty-five minutes to get to the only available airport, Kennedy International. From mid-Manhattan it takes about three-quarters of an hour and often twice as long in heavy traffic.

It would take probably half the people now using JFK *less* time to get to an airport among the Burlington pines than it now takes them to get to JFK. Present turnpikes and rapid rail facilities along existing rights of way *can* result in the most modern, swift transportation to a truly serviceable Tomorrow Airport.

This jetport could be located where growth, expansion, and development would be uninhibited, unhemmed in by residential and urban areas. It would, further, be infinitely more convenient to such additional cities as Philadelphia, Camden, Trenton, and so forth.

For heaven's sake, people fly from all over the United States to New York for JFK's multiple flights on multiple lines to all parts of the globe. Are the minutes involved in getting to a proper airport with proper facilities a determinant of whether they go to distant points or not?

Of course not.

The other argument as to the "unfeasibility" of such an airport comes from those who say it would "disrupt" existing air lanes and traffic patterns.

Well, now, isn't that too bad.

Is it *really* impossible to shuffle some air lanes instead of covering residential areas nearest New York City under acres of asphalt and concrete, under clouds of jet fuel fall-out, under an ever present blanket of thunderous jet noise?

It may take a bit of paper work, of course, on the part of a number of existing federal agencies, but is this an insurmountable problem? Suppose you have to shuffle the air lanes. So it takes a few more minutes to dogleg around Burlington Airport from Florida and Washington.

Is this a real reason to say it "can't" be done?

No.

Yet unimaginative men continue to push for impossible proximity. If they cannot have a site a few minutes closer to the city, then they won't budge toward any other solution.

These birds ought to be retired along with the DC-3s or stuffed in museums beside the extinct Ford trimotor planes.

You know, a few years ago an air traveler used to be able to land about ten minutes from the heart of Stockholm. Today you take a taxi to the edge of the city, and there at the passenger terminal, you board a bus for a near-hour ride out into the pinelands to their new Stockholm airport. The Swedes decided a jetport was to serve the people of Sweden, to serve the nation's needs. They decided that instead of having it blight their beautiful, lovely-to-live-in city, they would put their needed jetport where it could grow and be an asset instead of a menace, a detriment, a despoiler.

Everyone who must fly to Stockholm on business still does—more do every year. Everyone who flies to Sweden to see Sweden—more do every year—lands at this lovely new airport and drives through the magnificent Swedish countryside into a beautiful capital.

So, what's wrong with applying that approach here. Mr. President, Messrs. Governors, Messrs. Commissioners, Messrs. Aviation Industry Leaders?

5/1/67

I don't know anything about it, but it sounds like a marvelous idea.

A circular airport.

The United States Navy recently completed tests on the feasibility of a circular airport. A banked runway would form the perimeter. The advantages, tests showed, are multiple. The problem of ever longer runways is obviously solved because, as *The New York Times* helpfully points out, "A circle has no end."

Pilots who made test landings in assorted planes on General Motors' desert proving grounds said that the circular, banked runway gave so much landing stability that crosswinds no longer mattered. This being so, flight patterns for takeoff and landing in metropolitan areas can be devised over the least-inhabited areas, since landing or taking off into the wind won't be necessary.

The naval project officer said commercial pilots could learn the technique of landing on such a runway in "about five minutes, or one approach."

The amount of land required would be at least one-third less than that necessary for an equivalent conventional airport.

Since there is going to be no end to the increase in air traffic, and since the demand for airports in expanding population centers will keep growing, I hope the Feds will soon make this layout standard for all such new facilities.

Maybe even start converting some of the existing ones.

1/1/66

When Eastern Airlines introduced its new McDonnell-Douglas STOL (short takeoff and landing) aircraft, the accompanying fanfare would tend to make the unthinking think that this novel aircraft would contribute appreciably to lessening air problems in major cities, or in some other way make downtown urban centers more available.

How?

Just imagine how many of these sixty-four-passenger planes would be needed to move even one percent of the people who travel between Kennedy Airport and Manhattan, or Chicago's O'Hare Airport and the Loop, or Los Angeles Airport and Pershing Square. Instead of lessening air traffic this "advance," if numbers multiplied, would simply compound the air traffic problem in big city areas.

STOL obviously has its uses.

But none of them has anything to do with lessening

present air transportation problems and the need for new airports away from city centers.

Only rapid rails can do that.

Do you suppose one day someone who sees this simple truth will be in a position to start the ball rolling?

10/15/68

The British now charge substantially higher fees for planes taking off and landing during peak traffic hours at London airports.

The retiring head of the authority that runs them, Sir Peter Masefield, told *Forbes*: "Like many U.S. airports, Heathrow is not short of runways or facilities on a year-round, twenty-four-hour-a-day basis. The trouble is that everyone wants to land in peak hours, peak days, and peak months. We are starting to tax these golden hours."

If the difference in landing fees doesn't spread the traffic, Masefield continued, it can be widened until it is "more profitable for airlines to think in terms of landing during nonpeak hours."

Despite some inconvenience, we passengers have to go when the planes go to wherever it is we are going. Certainly, getting full use out of existing airports is infinitely preferable to building hundreds of millions of dollars worth of additional airports just to handle peak traffic.

5/1/72

Airport head tax.

Why not?

Throughout Europe every air traveler pays anywhere from a buck to a couple of dollars at most major modern airports. The take helps to finance the bonds that finance the building of them.

So what's wrong with that "use" tax if it helps to get

more of what we need more of—modernized air-traffic controls and additional airports?

2/1/69

Suggested advertising slogan for an airline:
    What a Way to Go!

2/15/69

The gut problem for our dangerously red-inked airlines is that fewer people rather than more have been taking to the air. Instead of the ascending-traffic chart line anticipated, there has been a sadly sagging one at a time when carrying capacity has soared.

Why?

Because the bread-and-butter backbone of passenger travel is not really the vacationer, who once in a while takes off to exotic places, but rather the businessman who's got to go from Chicago to Los Angeles and from New York to Atlanta and the like. When the recession hit and companies had to cut every cuttable cost, numberless traveling businessmen were grounded and told to telephone instead.

And in many cases it was found that the phone call worked (when the phone did) as effectively as, and at mucho less cost than, the personal visitation.

To overcome this "don't go—phone" philosophy is going to prove a bit difficult. For sure, though, the number of air travelers will climb again as more people begin to do more business. The rate and time of this climb will just be less and longer than those financing the airlines would like.

11/1/71

The airlines need more passengers.

So American Airlines is wooing them with full-page

ads about having put a piano in the middle of its 747 coach lounge.

In contrast, United headlines, "You're going to have to find a new excuse to leave your wife at home," and goes on to describe a special two-thirds off the price for wives along on business trips.

Now I am sure there is nothing better calculated to keep some businessmen off an airplane than the prospect of having to listen to a bunch of high passengers singing around a plinking piano . . . unless, for the same some businessmen (or another some), it's the prospect of taking their wives along on the next overnight trip to Peoria.

On the other hand, of course, if you like to play the piano and sing along as you wing along, American's obviously the way to go, or take United if your wife adores Peoria—or if you have a willing stand-in.

Somehow, I think United's probably got the best pitch —no matter how well-tuned American's piano.

1/15/72

The earnings bloodbath taken by United States airlines in the year just past and the dismal prospects for immediate improvement have raised questions in the minds of many about their economic survival. Last year the price tag placed on the top twelve lines by the stock market went from $3.9 billion to $3 billion. Altogether, the major United States airlines could be bought for the price of Avon stock with some $1.5 billion left over.

Is this dismalness justified?

I think not.

A recitation of airlines' woes indeed makes a diresome dirge—soaring labor costs, costly hijackings, vast costs for breaking in new 747-like equipment and huge financing costs of new craft, stalled traffic growth, lagging rate increases, additional ticket taxes, continuing proliferation of competition on lucrative routes, Justice Department finger wagging at cooperative attempts to lessen money-losing duplicated flights. Just to begin listing their woes is enough to ground one's spirits.

It is estimated the twenty-one scheduled United States airlines will show a collective loss for 1970 exceeding $130 million, with an added $20 million loss by ten supplemental lines.

So what case can be made for optimism?

Let's begin with a basic: Airlines are essential. Passenger trains are gone, and automobiling, for people, becomes more and more a problem and more and more expensive.

There are some able airline heads—the just-bounced George Keck was one. But hand wringers at airlines' helms will go the way of their companies' profits. Their successors will do better. Sufficient rate increases will be permitted, and there is enough prevailing intelligence in the Civil Aeronautics Board to direct and permit fewer flight duplications. Savings from vast, new, single-plane capacity will be felt effectively before the year is out. Sensible major airline consolidations will take place. Instead of encouraging a multiplicity of United States overseas carriers, who all lose money, by year's end there will be fewer and, once again perhaps, profitability for the survivors. (You don't notice France, the Netherlands, the Scandinavian countries, Italy, Germany, Japan, Britain, Belgium, or Switzerland each running two or three or four or five national overseas airlines, do you?)

Simply awesome, awful economic arithmetic, that is, unsupportably huge losses, is resulting in a reemergence of good sense on the corporate level and, most importantly, on the federal regulatory level.

The airlines have a future.

This is a good time to invest in a piece of them—when nobody seems to want 'em, and at a time when the industry will by 1971's end have no place to go but back up.

Reapers will succeed the weepers.

1/15/71

TOMBSTONES THAT MEMORIALIZE MONUMENTAL MISUSE OF MISSION AND MONEY

Port of New York Authority's Twin Towers.

3/15/71

In the Consumer's Corner

Meaningless warranties warrant consumer outrage.

Have you ever read one that comes with your new appliance, gadget, curtains, car, or most any other made thing you buy?

The word *guarantee* or *warranty* is writ big and bold and, as often as not, gold ink trellises surround the tiny print —which, as often as not, sets forth all the limitations which make most warranties a collection of words that don't say what they seem to. You and I know it isn't the broken wire or broken bit inside that costs, it's the time you take trying to get the store where you bought it or the company who made it to do the repairs. And mostly it doesn't include the cost of labor, the costliest part of all.

A few companies have grown big and ever bigger because their Word and words mean something. They make good when they've unintentionally done a bad—like J. C. Penney all of the time and Sears most of the time.

American Motors is breaking new warranty ground, and if it doesn't break them, it could make them.

Soon, and rightly so, it's going to be equally fraudulent to appear to guarantee when in fact the company doesn't.

Next time you buy something with a guarantee, either read the fine print or ask the seller just what it promises.

4/1/72

Say "inflation" at home these days and your wife will angrily wave a piece of red meat or a pack of green peas over her head and blast its cost. Damned will be the butcher, the baker, and the candlestick maker.

Gals, get off the poor merchants' backs.

You've got the wrong villain.

No matter what you may read about Huntington Hartford and his uniquely successful efforts to get rid of the money his family once made selling you groceries, today the big fooders as well as the little ones net a shamefully tiny profit on their whopping volume of business.

As Winn-Dixie's James E. Davis put it, "If a woman buys $10 worth of groceries in one of our stores and tips the bag boy a quarter, he's made more on the sale than we have. And we're the most profitable major chain."

Twenty years ago you spent 24.6 percent of your husband's paycheck for food. In 1960, 20 percent. Last year, 18 percent.

The food-pinching, penny-pinching French housewife spent 30 percent of her family's income for food.

For Japanese dolls it was 43 percent.

And if you really want to get sheared, try sharing food shopping with a Soviet housewife. *Over half* of the family income must go for food.

So ladies, pick another target. Your local supermarketer has to break his back to make a nickel.

1/1/67

I am sure all of us are familiar with many lines, from the plumb ones on ships to the love ones by gigolos. But have you heard of the "ear line"?

Well, your barber has.

I think Webster's dictionary could better define *speed* as the time between when your youngster gets one haircut and needs another. It is all connected with the ear line.

I discovered this wrinkle the hard way, sitting one afternoon while five youngsters got clipped. The shears flew, the hair blew, and the bill was astronomical. Within a couple of weeks of this costly occasion, I received word from one of the boys' teachers. My prodigy wasn't doing so well in oral quizzes. Maybe he wasn't hearing so well because his hair had grown over his ears, suggested the teacher.

At that point I finally caught on to what must be the first principle taught in barbers' Clipper College: "Take off as much or as little as they want, but above all *never* take much off above the ears." It is as difficult to get a barber to "lower" a kid's ears as it is easy to get him to raise his prices.

By studious attention to the ear line, barbers make sure

that haircuts don't last any longer than *your wife's* $50 hairdo by Mr. Kenneth.

I thought of one alternative. An old one. Inverting a suitable mixing bowl and applying the scissors from the sewing basket. The kids objected, however, that the hair style of Prince Charles had not yet become the mode in moppet America circles.

If Attorney General Kennedy really wants to save us laboring Americans from pocket picking by American business, he can shift his attention from those two-bit violators of the Sherman Antitrust Act and look into the ear line racket.

12/15/61

Probably the worst buy for the price (*any* price) are men's "good" raincoats.

A bunch of us sat in a wet football stadium not long ago, mostly wearing the same suntan Establishment-type fly-front raincoats that I guess cost anywhere from $35 to $135. After a bit we were nearly as wet inside as out. It seems after a few exposures the "waterproofing" disappears, and the cloth acts like a blotter, not a shedder. Our more sensible wives were mostly wearing clear plastic and had no such problem, and no such initial cost, either.

If it weren't for the fact that consumerism is currently out of hand, I could sure make a suggestion or two for a deserving target.

11/15/72

Since 1963 California has required TV repairers to be licensed. Before that, according to the industry's own estimates, Californians stood better than one in six chances of being gypped on repairs. The man who now heads the California state regulatory agency estimates that fraud has been reduced by one-third, and this has resulted in consumer savings of some $12 million a year.

In Denver auto repair shops require licensing, while in Connecticut and Delaware mechanics are licensed and regulated. The aim is to ensure some competence and make fraud more difficult.

Countless tests have been made demonstrating and documenting the standard of fraud and/or incompetence in auto repairs . . . cases of taking a car with a simple pre-prepared ailment to half a dozen or more garages and getting a different analysis and estimate of cost from each, some astronomical.

So, too, with TV repairs.

Be it fraud, as I think mostly it is, or be it incompetence, which certainly is widespread enough, California and Denver and Connecticut and Delaware have shown us how to do something about it.

We all manage to get subtly taken in enough ways every day not to have to put up with such crude, outright robbery.

11/15/67

While everyone is on the subject of safety and cars and carnage on the highways, I'd like to put in a plug for safety in another direction—the bathroom. I suppose in some homes it's used as often as the auto, and while I don't know the facts, I'll bet the accident rate is higher.

One principal cause is the frequent meeting of wet hands with glass bottles over hard sinks. This bloody (in both a literal and the British sense of the word) combination I am sure is a mainstay for the iodine-and-Band-Aid business.

Isn't it absurd that in this day of fabulous new containers of plastic and metals and paper and combinations thereof, companies still package bathroom items like toiletries, patent medicines, and prescription medicines in glass? The Monsanto Company is producing a new plastic of polyvinyl chloride—whatever that is—which is virtually as clear as glass and shatterproof as well. With tongue in cheek, an enthusiast for this new product suggested the other day that "We should have a slogan, 'Let's get the blood out of the bathroom,' and get even with the Glass Container Institute's advertisement, 'If you want to see it, put it in glass.' "

One can understand the partisanship of packaging industry partisans.

But the stupidity of using glass containers in the bathroom when alternatives are available does seem obvious.

4/15/66

The other day I learned something that I guess housewives learn early in life. It was a wallet-walloping experience.

Don't go supermarket shopping when hungry.

Recently, a fabulous new A&P opened up near home, and I went down around noon Saturday to pick up two wee, needed items.

But a funny thing happened on the way to where they lay. In passing the cold, fresh vegetable counters, I couldn't resist the crisp-looking chicory and, next to it, some beautiful endive, and what looked like just-husked corn on the cob. Not far off were some irresistible string bags of Little Neck clams and mouth-watering wheels and wedges of fabulous cheeses. Another refrigerated counter was loaded with assorted flavors of assorted ice creams and Good Humors. Nearby were cans and jars of fudge sauces, Marshmallow Fluff, and see-through bags of chocolate sprinkles. Plus numerous cakes and cookies of every variety. Then three different kinds of breakfast biscuits, and the pictures on the tubes looked the way breakfast biscuits should look.

It took the checkout man almost ten minutes to tote my take and take my stake.

The $2 mission turned into a $49.12 extravaganza.

My bursitis was in full bloom by the time I hefted the bags into the kitchen, and the headshaking disbelief on my wife's face as she emptied them finished off whatever ardor and appetite I had left.

We broke two knives, a fingernail, and two tempers trying with absolutely no success to open the clams; the corn was flavorless and tough; the jars of ice cream sauces grow dusty on the shelf for Storing Things Unused. Most of the cheeses shrink and shriek in the refrigerator.

The moral: Never, men, never go hungry to market.

6/15/68

Tilting Windmills

Along with all other mortals, from time to time I love to waste time. But not when writing editorials. This one, aimed at urging Congress to reduce sharply and eventually eliminate the capital gains tax, I realize in all probability is an exercise in futility. Tilting with windmills, however, is occasionally good for us pen knights. It reminds us that all our big fat opinions are not as powerful or portentous as we sometimes think.

Most investors are painfully familiar with the capital gains tax. The present 25 percent capital gains tax has two major, most serious faults. First, it acts to lock thousands and thousands of investors in securities which show appreciable appreciation. Two clamps do the trick. On the one hand, the investor must be willing to take a "loss" of 25 percent of his profit at the moment of sale, and on the other hand, he must anticipate a 25 percent profit in his new purchase just to come out even on the transaction. Conservative investors find such situations not too frequent. Thus the tax tends to stagnate investment when reasonable fluidity is the first mark of a healthy investment market.

Secondly, at a time when American business needs whetstone sharpening to compete in world markets, billions of investment dollars are needed to back new products, new research, new techniques. It can't all come from new sources. Redirected personal investments must constitute an important part of needed funds. The required constant expansion of our GNP won't come from a climate that encourages armchair coupon-clipping of current "sure things."

No one today amasses a fortune from salary. Income taxes rather effectively see to that. Only from capital gains can the needed investment billions be provided.

Recognizing this elementary truth, most European countries impose no capital gains taxes. They correctly reason capital is needed for the expansion, growth, and development of businesses, jobs, and living standards. These governments figure to "get theirs" from income and other direct taxes. They don't put a penalty on providing a vital national need— capital.

If it all makes so much sense, why do I find the expectation of its happening so unlikely? Because both the Admini-

stration and the vast majority of those in the Congress have
a not-unfounded fear of advocating a law which would seem
to favor "the rich." The incidental facts that such a tax revision would increase jobs as well as revenues and considerably enhance the nation's economic health have little bearing.
Reason and reasoning are poor reeds on which to lean when
election stumping against slogans about "soaking the rich."

4/15/62

I am an extravagant admirer of our telephone companies,
and *Forbes* has never stopped doffing its hat to their con-
sistent, remarkable progress. We even spoke up for digit
dialing when others were forming associations in protest.

But Picturephone is too much!

Hardly a housewife in America would dare answer her
phone during morning hours as she rushes around with hair
in curlers and a dusty housecleaning dress on.

What about the poor salesman who is calling in to the
office from the corner saloon instead of the home sickbed he
claims he is in?

Fathom for just a moment the Picturephone difficulties
of explaining to your wife that you won't be home 'til late
that night because of the pileup in the office and she sees a
martini-covered jukebox in the background.

What about the drive to put phones in the bathroom?

I tell you, Picturephone will set back phoning by decades. Half the time women will be scared to death to pick up
the phone until they first pick up their paint box.

Revenues will plummet.

When Picturephone really gets going, I'm going to get
bearish on phone stocks.

Which right now are still among the best buys available.

12/15/64

The National Association of Manufacturers would greatly further the causes it believes in if the NAM itself ceased to exist.

Unfortunately, a lot of people think NAM speaks for American business, that their policies and pronouncements reflect the opinions of most of management and the owners of business. Fortunately, in fact, they don't. Time and again able, foresighted business leaders have gone on NAM boards and committees with high hopes of broadening the association's perspective, but such attempts have thus far proven for the most part unsuccessful.

The NAM has done such an effective job that all it takes is their endorsement of a measure or a viewpoint to damn it in the eyes of legislators, large numbers of businessmen, and influential groups everywhere—and I'm not referring to the CIO or the professional left-wingers. As one who believes a national sales tax is necessary, I was discouraged at its prospects when the NAM came out in its favor. That'll make it tough to sell, no matter how logical.

It is harder to imagine a group rendering less service to the things it believes in than when the NAM gathers annually at the Waldorf-Astoria to pontificate on the issues of the day. The climax comes when an immense dais of white-tie-and-tailed executives is pictured throughout the nation's press looking down toward a ballroom filled with hundreds more in white tie and tails, listening to speeches about What This Country Needs.

The association actually consists of hundreds of companies and executives with deep conviction and sound thinking as individual entities. But by the time their resolutions percolate into mass adoption, the heavy hand of the so-called hard-headed school leaves them in the just-what-you'd-expect-from-reactionaries category. Maybe the fault lies with the "permanent secretariat" at headquarters, who must yes-sir

some of the heavy-dues-paying group that think the way to
sell their viewpoint is to hit 'em again harder. If the association would content itself with a useful job of fact finding, if it
had done what today the Committee for Economic Development does, a real service of value to free enterprise advocates
would be performed.

But today those who believe in free enterprise would be
far better off if the NAM would jump into one of the holes
it is constantly digging.

8/15/51

Isn't it incredible how little governments are doing to end the
nightmare of skyjacking?

Particularly our own.

Imagine our government sabotaging as best it could the
International Airline Pilots one-day strike intended to force
more forceful approaches to end the mess.

The International Air Transport Association meets
often enough when there's a rate war. Why can't it meet immediately, and promptly agree that no airline will serve any
country which doesn't return within twenty-four hours skyjackers, their boodle, the plane, passengers, and crew to the
country of origin?

Since the death penalty is no longer possible, *real* life
sentences should be mandatory for skyjackers.

I hope the next time the International Airline Pilots
strike is soon and even more successful and longer—unless
governments and their airline operators get cracking on this
murderous outrage.

8/15/72

While the number of plane hijackings is down, there are still
too many. *Any* is too many.

Why can't the appropriate federal agency or agencies

simply issue a dictum that any hijacked plane landing at any United States airport to refuel in the course of its unauthorized flight *must* have its tires shot dead immediately. No ifs, ands, or buts.

Since so many of those bizarre takeovers seem to involve lengthy flight and refueling, this edict should stop them. Every would-be hijacker would know that the decision wasn't in the hands of the pilot, or the passengers, or subject to bargaining.

Combined with mandatory jail sentences, mandatory tire shooting should help end the horrendous practice.

7/15/70

If letters could kill, I'd sure as shooting be as dead right now as effective gun-registration legislation is dead in the Congress.

Here recently, I wrote in support of a law that would require the registering of firearms and the licensing of users. The editorial concluded with these three questions:

"Who is it that blocks such legislation?

"Why do they block it?

"How are they *able* to stop it?"

Boy, I got the answers!

To date 123 letters of varying degrees of vehemence—including four subscription cancellations—have set forth the case of those opposed to such a measure. Most of these letters were from men of responsibility in business, including a number of corporate heads.

Those against such legislation have a genuine sense of outrage at what they feel would be a limitation of their individual freedom. Equally, they feel that guns in the hands of the citizenry are a valuable safeguard should domestic communists ever attempt to take over the government by force. In the opinion of many of the letter writers, the first thing a dictator-minded government would do, if they knew who had guns and where they were, would be to confiscate them. Most make the point that the fact of gun registration has not cut down the incidence of criminal gun use in such very strict gun-law towns as New York.

While I personally am not persuaded by the rationale, it certainly has been made very clear who it is that blocks such legislation, why they do it, and how they do it. By exerting the rights of free citizens to be heard, by feeling strongly and expressing themselves unequivocally to all who might have a hand in legislation, those opposed to stronger gun laws continue to succeed in blocking such bills, even though the polls show 89 percent of the citizenry favor passage.

If there is anything the rest of us should learn from this experience, it's the enormous effect that individual citizens can have if they raise their voices and write as they feel to those who make our laws.

8/15/68

Who would, could sensibly oppose a *reasonable* program for some degree of tax credit for college tuition?

In point of fact, those who now have it the toughest are the family breadwinners who are earning too much to qualify on a poverty basis for scholarship aid, but too little to meet the heavy burden of their youngster's college costs. Tuition, board, lodging, books, clothes, and assorted sundries for a college year are figured to average over $2,000. If there is more than one child in college—and the average American family now has 2.39 children—the strain on the family income, even if it is well over $10,000 a year before taxes, is frequently prohibitive.

A number of proposals to permit a tax credit are in the congressional hopper, some of them having been introduced for many years. It is high time the advocates got together on one measure and put it through. The postwar baby crop is now of college age, and the squeeze between rising costs and larger numbers is really on and really hurting.

With a President and a Congress and a people all sympathetic to the family financial problem and all warmly committed to the value of higher education, it surely should be possible this year to enact a meaningful college tuition tax-credit measure.

4/15/65

This country is engaged in a vast spending program of billions to provide the military might necessary to guard the free world from successful conquest by communists. We are spending additional billions to shore up the economies of our allies, so that they won't fall victims to the Reds through economic collapse and internal chaos.

But these great efforts must be paid for. Washington, though it prints money, doesn't make money.

The remaining most logical source of substantial new revenue is a national sales tax. It would not be a new or shocking thing. Today's 20 percent tax on luxury items, the excise taxes on liquor, gasoline, cigarettes, and many manufactured articles are nothing more than a hit-or-miss, unbalanced national sales tax that most people don't know they are paying. Such a tax, exempting food, drugs, and possibly shelter, would raise the great sums needed; it would be paid by all, and all would know it; it would not be so difficult to collect and administer that a vast new bureaucracy was needed; we have, in effect, a hodgepodge national sales tax now in the form of excises; and there is ample precedent for such a tax both in our own country on the state and city level, and in other countries on a national level. Canada has had a 10 percent retail sales tax which runs their government on a balanced budget and has enabled them to reduce substantially their national debt.

There is no such thing as a popular tax or an easy one. We have the job to do, and a national sales tax on the retail level provides the means of doing it.

8/15/51

Lawyers are not supposed to advertise.

So how do they acquire a Name and the clients that a Name attracts? They run for public office or enter politics on the appointive level and get their names all over the paper and TV, mostly for free.

On more esoteric grounds, some lawyers are seeking to change the prohibition against lawyers' advertising. The rest of us might do well to support the change on the proposition that the public interest would better be served if there were fewer lawyers in public office.

The great majority of lawmaking bodies in this country are lawyers. They pass laws by the bucketful, which require lawyers by the bucketful, who collect bucketsful of coin from the rest of us for advice on how to comply or how to avoid complying with all the stuff they pass.

I say, let 'em advertise like any other souls, and we'll all be better off.

11/1/70

If the Administration and the Congress want to give the economy a pep shot of real proportions, they could initiate a conversion to the metric system for the United States. We've got to get with the rest of the world sooner or later, in scales of weight and length anyway. Just think what the necessary conversions might mean to machine tool companies and textbook publishers and printers—to mention only a couple of the many to benefit measurably.

After all, if the English can give up their ancient monetary pounds and shillings for the decimal system, and the Swedes can shift from driving on the left to the right, Americans can at least learn to measure up by the common, commonsense metric standards prevailing in the rest of the world.

4/1/72

Compulsory arbitration.

It has to come.

At least and at the minimum in certain publicly essential industries where the monopoly power of unions is so total as to make a mock of "negotiations." Like transportation, including ports and shipping.

Ditto police, firemen, sanitation, transportation shutdowns in cities.

Ditto utilities, such as the strike that blacked-out Britain during last winter and nearly broke the back of organized labor there.

Compulsory arbitration has properly been anathema to management and unions, and it should remain so *except* where the monopoly of the union is total and the service or industry is essential.

1/15/72

Some 150 years ago the Swedes created the office of ombudsman, a man with the power to investigate any citizen's grievance against the state. His job is to ensure fair treatment to all. He investigates and recommends. He has neither legislative nor administrative powers, but it's a rare day that his "suggestions" are not followed.

Since Denmark took up the idea ten years ago, it has

gained support all over the place. Norway, New Zealand, Britain. Widespread enthusiasm for ombudsmen now exists in Canada, India, Ireland, and the United States.

It's a great, good notion for our time, when government at every echelon grows and grows and grows, when bureaucracy enters into ever more facets of every man's everyday life.

In the simplicity of the idea is much of its strength. As a practical matter, for any citizen the phrase "You can't fight City Hall" is an absolute truth.

But the ombudsman can.

Quickly.

Effectively.

His concern is not with the letter of the law but with the intent.

His very existence tends to keep bureaucrats on the ball, and his power to focus the spotlight of publicity on his recommendations should ensure that the individual doesn't get ground fine in the machinery or bureaucracy.

Possibly on the vast federal level it wouldn't work.

But in the big cities it certainly should. On the state level it should.

Alert governors and caring mayors can give meaning to their multiple speeches about concern for all the people by creating the office of ombudsman in their bailiwicks and appointing an outstanding Good Man from among their constituents to this new post of great importance.

12/1/66

Fifteen years ago an Australian engineer designed a single eating utensil, called the splayd, combining the functions of knife, fork, and spoon in one. The thing is eminently sensible, fully functional, patented in fifty-two countries, and manufactured on a royalty basis in twenty-five.

Wouldn't you think it would sell by the multimillions? That most everywhere there is eating done, it would be in demand?

But it's not.

Why, do you suppose?

4/15/72

With the vote for eighteen-year-olds a fact of national political life, the question has been raised as to why undergraduates cannot vote in their college community, since it's their residence while they are students.

To permit that would be a dangerous travesty on the residency requirements. Communities raise almost all of their revenues by property tax. To a substantial degree, so do states. Students pay none, nor do the institutions they attend. Yet sophists argue the student vote should help elect local officials—even students themselves—to direct the police and public schools of the community where they happen to be attending college.

That would be as wrong as it could be.

Ask any undergraduate, "Where's home?" and he doesn't answer "Kent" or "Berkeley" or "Princeton" or "Ann Arbor"—home is where his family lives, where he lives when he isn't away at college.

It shouldn't take the wisdom of a Solomon to arrive at that conclusion, and voting residence should be, must be, where home really is.

8/1/71

For those so vehemently and violently pushing, pounding, bleating, and beating for women's liberation in the United States, I'd recommend they check out the way the women of Italy have achieved their liberation.

Neither laws nor the surface submissiveness by the ladies of Italy toward the men of Italy has a darn thing to do with the realities. In law their women have little or no rights, status, standing. Ostensibly and ostentatiously, the men rule their women with all the tyranny that the most rabid male chauvinist could desire.

But, and I do mean *but*—

If you've ever been to Italy, you know from the first instant who *really* rules country, home, and hearth. The enveloping, unadulterated, unending, overwhelming love of Italian mothers for their children, particularly their sons, enables them to rule the roost absolutely and completely. If ever there is, was, has been, or will be a matriarchal society, it is, was, has been, and will continue to be Italy.

In other words, girls, the Italian ladies are a million miles ahead of those of you who want mere equality. Why fight for, settle for that when by loving us ever more and more you can be more than equal?

You can be in total charge.

The battle cry for Women's Lib ought to be *"Viva Italia!"*

10/15/70

Headline from *The New York Times*:

ROME'S POLICE ACT TO PROTECT
WOMEN TOURISTS FROM ROMEOS

Do they think women tourists go to Rome just for the ruins?

8/1/72

There's an emergency looming in air.

One of New York State's commissioners on human

rights has officially opined that airlines which require stewardesses to quit at ages lower than the standard retirement
in other industries are guilty of discrimination.

This commissar bird is of the opinion that it's a human
right for a once-young gal to go right on stewardessing until
she is an unsteady granny.

What about the human rights of the passengers?

Airlines only really got off the ground when they got
the bright idea of featuring young, pretty stewardesses. Passengers found the sight of such most stimulating. In tur-
bulent weather it's comforting to be told to fasten your belt
by a lovely young lady. Surely, tremulous passengers would
find little reassurance and no inspiration from an old crone
tottering up and down the aisle.

Setting a young age limit for plane girls is discrimina-
tory?

Re-diculous.

These famed lovelies of the airlines are among the industry's greatest assets. They shouldn't be jeopardized, nay,
wiped out, by the mere expression of a way-out opinion of
some aging commissioner.

5/1/66

It was high time somebody blew the whistle on the myriad
charities whose solicitors annually gather $1.5 billion for the
support of their activities. Businessmen and businesses large
or small are always prime targets for the over 100,000 voluntary health and welfare agencies now in operation.

It is not the giving that bothers the conscientious givers,
but the unanswered question of how much of each donated
dollar ends up being spent for the purposes outlined. A recently completed Rockefeller Foundation–financed study of
the whole problem points out that "almost no carefully

evaluated information is available on how voluntary agencies spend the $1.5 billion that the public now entrusts to them each year." The study group, headed by Lindsley F. Kimball, estimates that approximately 25 percent, or $375 million, of the money contributed goes to administrative overhead, fund raising, public and professional information costs. While some agencies claimed only 5 percent went for this purpose and others admitted as much as 57 percent, the accounting procedures of most agencies are so vague, slipshod, or misleading that fund-raising costs are well-nigh impossible to determine.

The committee report further states, "The predominant desire of the agencies too frequently is for self-perpetuation to the detriment of overriding public interests." Most of us can recall the wide-reaching fund-raising effort, for instance, of The National Foundation for Infantile Paralysis, particularly because under its auspices the cure emerged—Salk vaccine. But with its purpose in large measure accomplished, this foundation didn't wind up headquarters: It simply dropped its name and expanded its purposes.

Says the Rockefeller committee, "It does not take over 100,000 voluntary agencies . . . to provide private health and welfare services in the United States." The committee goes on to recommend appointment of an independent national commission to make a "thorough evaluation" of the agencies and the development of uniform accounting and financial reporting.

A voluntary effort to bring order and responsible accounting to the whole field is infinitely preferable to any federal regulation. Yet so long as contributions to these causes are tax deductible, the government has a reason to move into the area in response to growing citizen irritation.

I can think of one approach that might lend substantial

impetus to voluntary collective action along the outlines in the Rockefeller study. Before giving as a business and/or as a businessman to any charity, ask for a copy of a certified accounting of funds previously raised showing clearly what went for overhead and what went for the objectives stated. No compliance, no contribution.

As one who has often canvassed for causes, I have heard many quite imaginative reasons for not giving by those who didn't want to. The above would be a most useful response both for those who give and those who don't.

9/15/61

The Fourth of July's most appropriate, predominating theme is the American flag. No self-respecting town-hall or town-park orator would dream of waving his finger from any platform not bunted in red, white, and blue to mark our national birthday.

Which brings to mind a minor but major matter that has long bothered me—why, to mark the passing of our greatest national heroes, greatest figures, do we *lower* the flag half way down the pole?

In the war that won us freedom, as in all the others fought to keep it, men died to *raise* that flag.

Are there not perhaps more appropriate ways to mourn . . . perhaps a black streamer on the flag staff?

On the Fourth of July 190 years ago we ran up the flag to celebrate the fact that no one any longer could make us lower it. On Memorial Day and memorial days is it suitable to bring it down?

7/1/66

For two decades I have struggled with less than success against our offsprings' incredibly constant use of those truly meaningless words *y'know* and *I mean*.

You know what I mean—I mean, you know.

These asinine phrases occur more frequently in the conversation of most people than four-letter words in the mouths of drill sergeants. At least the drill sergeant conveys his meaning without a lot of you knows and I means.

If you want to be appalled, try counting the number of times these vacuous words occur in your next conversation.

4/1/71

Observations—
On Target

What follows is a verbatim transcript of an interview that Peter Joseph had with me in 1972 and subsequently published in a book, *Good Times: An Oral History of America in the Nineteen Sixties* (1973). Quoting from the *Good Times* dust jacket: "The Nineteen Sixties were years of tragedy and trauma for America. But if they were the worst of times, they were also, ironically, the best of times—exhilarating, event-filled, personality-packed years that excited and enriched us as much as they sobered us and brought us to the edge of chaos. *Good Times* is a vibrant account of those years—'a fantastic living tapestry,' *Publishers' Weekly* calls it—told in the words, gathered especially for this book, of the people who made it happen."

". . . A WHOLE NEW SET OF VALUES"

It's simply that it's no longer essential to grub for material things. The success of capitalism has created such a degree of prosperity, not just in things, to where now young people don't have to think, "How am I going to earn a living?" They can think, "How am I going to live?" The economic pressure is off them. This is the success of capitalism.

The whole purpose used to be . . . the thesis I was taught in college was that the measure of a civilization was when people could afford to be interested in the arts and finer things of life. They didn't have to sweat for their daily bread. Now the average Indian in India today, his total concentration is getting enough food to stay alive. In this country the concern of more young people—and not just those in college—is doing something they enjoy doing. They don't want to be rich per se, because what the hell do you do with riches when you have them?

I don't feel the feeling against capitalism is stronger than before. Remember, there have been revolutions since the Industrial Revolution against the conditions that result from capitalism. Free enterprise, which basically is private ownership. In other words, you can own your own home; it doesn't belong to the government. That is, in essence, what you mean by free enterprise. They've got to realize that capitalism is an essential ingredient of what we think of as personal freedom. What they are against are abuses of an economic system that is far from perfect.

But when weighed against the so far available alternatives, I think they have to come down and decide that the more truly liberal, the more truly liberated a person is, the more he will come to realize that what he wants is to reform the evil, not do away with the system. Because the alternative systems so far require the Big Brother dictatorial approach. Everybody owns the automobile factor, so there are none in Russia. Or there might be three. And nobody has a car.

Part of the freedom that youth values is to get in and go, to take their own camper and live in it if they want, instead of living in New York in their family's apartment. But their freedom also relates to a thing that we happen to have much of—campers. The whole emphasis today is great—that kids just don't care about cars. That isn't the big status symbol it was in my generation. The kids have educated us. We've graduated from the big car syndrome to where we are more concerned with preserving a forest.

They don't have the same set of end values. They want their own lives to be useful. And where it can be very useful now is in these voluntary efforts to halt abuses. Ralph Nader has got them turned on. They feel, gee, this is an avenue of achieving a better life for more people. Putting an end to exploitation, putting an end to the phoniness of business. And others just want to do their own things: commune, or write, or think, or just enjoy. But you can get a surfeit of any one of those. You just can't make a life of total pure thought. You've just got to make the lean-to, you've got to make the campfire. The young people today, they don't measure success by money. As a matter of fact, the rich are sort of looked down on as people who are imprisoned by their things. They're not free to rove and to roam and to live and to do what they want to do. They've introduced a whole new set of values, but that doesn't mean they want to do away with capitalism. What do you substitute? What do you put in its place? There has to be some way of making things. You know, you can't go back to caveman days. There are too many people and not enough caves.

From where I sit, it seems to me youth are accomplishing. They are doing much to rectify the wrongs they are concerned with. And tomorrow there will be other things that need rectification. Like ecology. It has not succeeded poverty, but it's a new concern. Immensely important. Nobody gave it a thought before. We were all concerned with getting out our magazines, not concerned with who threw them where, and how you got rid of them, how they got recycled. Everything was inexhaustible. It was who made the quickest buck. Well, there's a new awareness.

This generation has achieved far more than they think they have. They think nothing has changed. Changes have been enormous, but the impact of it isn't immediately visible. You know, if you want to get something done today, and God, it hasn't been done in six months, it's the end of the world! But it isn't. It's the beginning of a new world.

10/15/73

Everybody loves to back up his opinion by quoting "an expert." In after-dinner arguments when one propounds an opinion with no facts in support, quoting an expert in the field is always supposed to be the clincher.

Experts?

What is an expert anyway? One familiar definition describes him as "anybody fifty miles from home." As is usually the case with old saws, there is a vast amount of truth in this one. Stock market experts are by no means the only vulnerable group. Trials have long been highlighted by "experts" giving exactly opposite testimony on handwriting, medical analysis, and psychiatry. Scientists, supposedly dealing only in the observable or demonstrable, are the most vulnerable of the lot. Witness the apoplectically expressed differences among them on the subject of fallout, shelters, and related matters.

In fact, the term *expert* is all too often a bit of flattery bestowed by speaker committee chairmen for the after-luncheon speech at the weekly Podunk Service Club meet-ing. The knowledgeable, of course, know that such a flowery introduction is payment in lieu of cash for the expenses of getting to Podunk in the first place.

What's an expert? I read somewhere that the more a man knows, the more he knows he doesn't know. So I sup-pose one definition of an expert would be someone who doesn't admit out loud that he knows enough about a subject to know he doesn't really know much.

Personally, I'm still inclined to award the title to those whose opinions agree with my own.

12/1/62

Experts kill me.

Economic experts, that is.

Corporations, foundations, publications, and govern-ments pay them by the bucketful, and they fill buckets with forecasts that change more frequently than white-collar workers do shirts.

Being in this business, I read faithfully what all the highly educated prognosticators say daily, weekly, and monthly about the outlook for the next few weeks, the next few months, and the next few years.

"What Lies Ahead" is the usual title.

"What Lies" would often be a more appropriate head-ing.

If you take all those quoted during the last few months in *The New York Times* on the subject of the economic outlook, it's positively flabbergasting how the trend runs. Some days they split down the middle as to whether things are going up or down. Other day's everybody's mouthing in the same direction, all up or all down.

If women's hemlines changed as rapidly as an economist's forecast, the fashion people and the textile industry would be more profitable than any other. As a matter of fact, if all the country's economists were laid end-to-end, they still wouldn't reach a conclusion.

The danger is not that they don't know any more than the rest of us about what's going to happen.

You and I all know they don't.

The danger is that Important People In Government often act on the premise that there are "expert economists." On the basis of their forecasts, the Feds fiddle around with tax rates, interest rates, and all sorts of controls.

Maybe before they get the economic machinery all screwed up, we ought to tell the Washington wheels that there is really no such thing as an expert economist.

(Modesty prevents me from naming the only exception which came immediately to *my* mind.)

6/1/67

Swedes are not noted for a tongue-in-cheek approach to life. Of all the unlikely lands in which to find humor on a national scale, it's Sweden. And of all the Swedish groups least likely to be associated with wit on an international scale, it's the noble Nobel Academy.

But this year they won the Laugh Laurels uncontestedly.

They have just awarded the Alfred Nobel Prize in Economic Science to two economists.

What for?

In the words of *The New York Times*: "As a result of the mathematical formulas worked out by Professors Frisch and Tinbergen, as well as others, economic policy-makers are able to achieve a closer approach to certainty in determining what economic buttons to press to achieve certain economic goals, such as faster growth."

The Button-Keeping Place must be the world's best kept secret.

But this award in the name of the dead old gunpowder maker must strike him as a hot one—if nuances of heat are detectable in his present habitat.

12/1/69

When my father was outraged by some really bad violation of business ethics, he would brand it "unconscionable."

I think it appropriate to use that word to describe the present situation whereby a corporate employee forfeits all equity of time and money in his company's pension plan should he leave voluntarily, be fired, or the company go under.

Soundly conducted retirement plans are funded annually. The government encourages their existence by making the corporate contribution a fully deductible business expense. Yet if a man, after ten or more or less years, shifts jobs by desire or necessity, he usually loses all.

That is not right.

It is heartening to see President Nixon pushing legislation that will safeguard employees' contributions in cases of bankruptcy or misuse of such funds. I hope the measure ultimately will include some form of vested interest in individual pension benefits so that if a man should be fired or leave a company after a certain period of time, he can take at least a reasonable part of his equity along with him.

8/15/70

Remember how shocked we all were as students to read about the barbarity of child labor in the early factories of the Industrial Revolution?

Would you believe that *today* throughout the United States tens of thousands of kids from seven to eleven, twelve, thirteen spend from dawn to dark, twelve hours a day, at the stooped, back-bent, hard, hard, hard labor of picking crops—for relatively few cents an hour?

Not just all summer long. Often they start with the season's beginning, which is long before schools close, and continue to season's ending, long after schools begin.

It's incredibly outrageous, inhuman, and almost inexplicable that this exists on a scale and under conditions that equal if not exceed the long-ago factory barbarities of mid-Victorian times.

If there's any conscience left in us these days, let's stir our stumps enough, each in his own state, to find out if this is permitted. And don't be fobbed off by assurances about inspections and standards and so forth.

Take a look-see at some dawn's early light.

Or at twilight's last gleaming.

Here, U.S.A.

Near home. Our homes.

Today. Not a century ago.

8/15/71

It's all well and good and understandable for people in high places and every place to be sometimes mad at the press, at newspapers and magazines with which they disagree, at pornography, at press sensationalism and press sex-sationalizing. But the people must never, never permit ire in high places to threaten, to curb the freedom of the press.

What's the very first step taken by every dictatorship

since history has been recorded? The prohibition of free speech, the curbing and elimination of a free press.

A *perhaps* unintended but insidious assault on the freedom of the press to probe, to inform is the effort by the Department of Justice to subpoena journalists and force them to reveal sources of information.

It's usually no easier for the press to dig out crookedness and corruption in places of power than for law enforcement agencies to do so. Just as informers for assorted and usually unsavory reasons are the source of leads on crime, so too are informers with assorted motives often the people who provide reporters with information on skulduggery.

The decision by a federal court upholding a journalist's right to protect his sources is immensely valuable to all the people of this country. To let rage and pique at the press, for good and bad reasons, lead to a curbing of enterprising reporting would be disastrous to the freedom of us all.

"Our liberty depends on the freedom of the press, and that cannot be limited without being lost"—Thomas Jefferson.

5/1/70

In a harrowing factual roundup on the truly scary spread of hard-drug addiction among the young and very young, New York City's Congressman Charles Rangel recently observed, "The pharmaceutical companies won't invest large funds to develop a nonaddictive heroin substitute since there's no profit in it for them."

Why?

Why not?

I suppose the unthinking (which includes most of us much of the time) tend to think that a company that makes something that cures illness and prevents disease makes it nearly free and freely available. It's all part of the utter rot that there's something wrong with profit, and particularly profiting from pain.

How in 'ell can any drug company spend millions looking for products to fill a need, if it has no profit from the products already developed that fill a need? Cars are absolutely essential for most of us—but do we expect General Motors to operate as a charity? So, too, housing. Ditto clothing. Food. And so on and on.

It's a chilling challenge, this murderous hard-drug epidemic. Getting hooked is apparently appallingly easy and for the most part proving almost incurable.

Any drug company that can develop any sort of answer to the hard-drug menace should find governments on every level, as well as individuals who can afford it, glad to pay a price that should include a profit—a very, very sizable profit. No matter what the price, it would be small compared with the soaring cost in lives, hospital and correctional institutional incarceration, theft, violent crimes—a cost that is in the billions.

A company making a few million from finding an answer that saves us thousands of young lives and billions of dollars should be and shall be blessed not blasted.

2/15/72

IN REAL PERIL

Our universities, public and private.

And I don't mean from student strikes and campus turbulence. Nor do I refer to undergraduate psychotics dedicated to the literal destruction of the country's colleges. The latter are identifiable and removable cancers, and the former have usually sprung from undergraduates' strong feelings, right or wrong, about wrongs they want righted.

No, the perils to the great learning centers of our land are far more complex, far more difficult to cure. Universities must have money to exist, and the last couple of years that necessitous commodity has come into short supply.

The freedom and vehemence with which undergraduates these days express their concerns have antagonized many of their older countrymen whose labor produces the taxes and the gifts that support these institutions.

Long hair and bizarre dress have produced more in the way of fallout than mere dandruff. This adult reaction may be as absurd as the clothes and beards students wear, but it has had grievous impact on the public support which is prerequisite to political appropriations and much alumni benevolence.

On top of this, endowment funds have shrunk with the market.

Other operational costs have climbed as much or more for colleges as they have for families and companies.

American business is in a profit squeeze, but, thank goodness, almost all businesses have had some profit to be squeezed. Universities, however, have no such thing, and such rainy day reserves as endowments can meet only an infinitesimal part of their annual costs.

It will be a very dark hour—and that dark hour is nearer at hand than we realize—should many colleges close their doors in bankruptcy, should others have to curb or cut out assorted departments and dismiss those who spend their lives on things of mind and matters that matter.

It behooves everyone who loves this land of freedom, who can look beyond his nose, who really understands that our greatness lies not in things but in freedom in the true sense, to wake up and help stanch the tide of misunderstanding and hatred that threatens to diminish our universities.

8/15/70

At today's prices for medicines, doctors, and hospitals—if the latter are available at *any* price—only millionaires can afford to be hurt or sick and pay for it.

Very few people want socialized medicine in the United States.

But pressure for it is going to appear with the same hurricane force as the demand for pollution control if the medicine men and hospital operators don't take soon some Draconian measures to heal themselves.

A study recently submitted to the Senate Finance Committee puts in black and white what every person who's sampled the wares knows.

At the present rate of doctor fees and hospital costs under Medicare-Medicaid plans, the charges to the states and the Feds (us taxpayers), we are shoveling in billions of dollars with nothing but escalation in sight.

The staff report highlights a few recommendations:

• Have an advisory board of actuaries and underwriters assist in setting up a schedule of fixed allowances for surgical and medical care for each of the nine regions in the nation.

• Establish a new Medicaid fraud-and-abuse unit that would monitor state programs.

• Create an "incentive reimbursement" system for doctors, hospitals, and nursing homes so those that provided the same care less expensively would be rewarded.

• Inform patients of payments made to their doctors to curb payments for services not performed.

The American Medical Association or someone had better start to crack down on those who are cheating on the intent and spirit and probably the letter of the laws establishing Medicare and Medicaid. Hospital associations had better start turning over the operation of their facilities to men who are experienced in running such businesses as motels and hotels.

Crazy? Not at all. Prescriptions for medicine and scheduling in operating rooms and all that medical gut stuff is the staff doctors' business. But the business of feeding and housing and heating and bedding and plumbing and all the rest of it needs the businesslike approach of those in the bedding business—hoteliers and moteliers.

If we do not act, and very soon, the present system will have us near broke.

The government, by popular demand, will take over.

That can only make the whole problem worse.

3/15/70

The United States is selling less and less abroad, importing more and more. This trade imbalance grows worse and worse, depreciating the dollar as a world currency and contributing to growing unemployment here.

With a full head of steam, we are sailing down the same course that has brought Britain to her economic knees.

There is no simple cure, no single villain.

Indisputably, soaring wage costs—including the can and aluminum agreements, and the looming steel and copper settlements, or around 31 percent over a three-year period—are the biggest single factor in making American products unexportably expensive, uncompetitive in the increasingly competitive marketplaces of the world. Not only are union wage stickups at fault—unvisioned managements satisfied only with the domestic market play a part in the problem.

Exporting our knowhow has been a prime revenue producer in recent years, to the point where it is now being used against us—by lower-labor-cost countries, who now sell to us for less what our machines and our brains taught them to make so well and efficiently.

Is the answer then to fence ourselves off from world trade and "protect" our large domestic market?

Such a course, widely pursued, would plunge our own country and the rest of the free world into depression and political chaos. Cocoon living on this complex globe is utterly impossible, and to attempt it is demonstratively mad.

What course then?

The situation is far from hopeless. There are things to be done today, things that can be started now for impact tomorrow.

Some lesser but important ones: Encourage the administration in its present exploration of negating antitrust laws where American companies might unite to compete in foreign markets. Most everywhere around the globe American companies face the challenge of government-supported cartels that compete for every sort of market, from services to construction to computers to the things for sale at a Woolworth counter. Japan Inc. is the prize example of the extraordinary success of government-business collaboration in the world marketplaces. For us to compete abroad in many places, our companies must be permitted to unite where it will help their competitive stance. Such collaboration obviously begins only where our own shores end. Within our own country, effective antitrust enforcement remains essential, must not be eroded.

Secondly, cut out toe-dancing with the countries that unfairly shut us out of their domestic markets. Here the government had better start applying the golden rule, albeit with a golden glove.

Thirdly, apply meaningful tax incentives to those companies who make things here and sell 'em there.

As to what we *should* do about enormous wage settlements, that's one thing.

What we *can* do about them is another.

No administration can go on doing nothing about the matter. If wage settlement guidelines are unpalatable or un-workable, then wage-price freezes must be considered.

If, politically, no one can be found to try it, the only alternative is arbitration—compulsory arbitration.

The Lord only knows from whence will come a labor-and-management-applauded panel, but it'll have to be sought and tried.

The essential goal of improving our position in the world marketplaces is possible. We just have to wake up—soon—to the fact that it's something we had better get right busy doing something about.

Now.

7/1/71

It's absolutely criminal the way people charged with unmur-derous crime can and do stay jailed for weeks and months and sometimes years before their cases come to trial or judg-ment.

It's wonderful and quite extraordinary the way the present Chief Justice of the United States is leading the fight to speed the day of judgment for those charged with breaking the law.

Undue delay every day diminishes the chance for actual justice for the individual charged. Crime is little deterred when the day of judgment, the day of reckoning lies in a relatively distant future.

If this Chief Justice can effect real court-and-jail reform, he will have done more to make this, in fact, a Land of Liberty and Justice for All than anyone since the Founding Fathers penned that noble intention.

4/15/71

That our jails are a crime against society as well as criminals has been oft and powerfully said by the knowledgeable as well as by the emotionally outraged.

In the early days of this country, you know, there were few jails. There was crime, probably in the same proportions as today. Punishment was a day or two in the stocks in the town square supplemented occasionally by the whip. Both are gone and of little feasibility in and for our times.

But jailing people in the circumstances now existing is so self-defeating for the greatest percentage, so costly in cash, and so productive of further crime against society—never mind the god-awful impact on the inmates—that it just must, has to, change.

For endless years before Attica, study after study concluded that literal locking up for any length of time is probably the least productive, most counterproductive way to punish, reform, rehabilitate.

There are alternatives, not all as impractical as in some backward lands, where in lieu of jail they still chop the hand off the thief. Sweden has not only minimum security institutions where it best fits the person (not the crime), but prisoners are permitted to go to work every day and to the jug in between times—unless they merit an occasional weekend at home.

There isn't a city in this nation which couldn't put qualifying prisoners usefully to tasks that so sorely need doing in terms of the cleanup of parks, the reclamation of land and streams; in just the washing up, sprucing up of city and countryside. There are a hundred ways such man- (and woman-) power could help in fighting pollution, in salvaging the ecology. Britain now has prisoners building modern prisons—a work they can take an interest in. California has used probationers to fight forest fires.

The cost of keeping a man in jail is very, very high. Tuition at these schools and graduate schools for crime and dehumanization exceeds that of most ordinary schools and universities on a per capita basis.

Cities, states, and even the Feds haven't remotely enough money to tackle all the sorely needed public works and projects that need no skill, only direction.

If each state and the federal prisons started to classify prisoners by temperament and repeated crimes of physical violence, they'd find upwards of 80 percent don't need maximum security. Prisoners, and all of society, could benefit to the maximum from their doing things that need doing.

This isn't soft-hearted stuff.

It's hard-headed and foresighted, and it is being done in some, but too few, places.

Our Attorney General, John Mitchell, has already spoken out on the degree to which our penal system promulgates more crime and hardly any cures. He has started trying to roll the ball.

We'd all gain by lending a hand.

10/15/71

More and more Americans seem to be getting madder and madder about the ever multiplying numbers which they must carry to live—or at least to prove they are alive. There used to be a time when all a man had to know was five numbers for his telephone and his license plate number. Then came Social Security. Later, for we ancient warriors of World War II, there were serial numbers and rifle numbers to be remembered. But now it takes ten numbers to dial home or the office from only a few miles away, and the latest is an unzippy string of numerals to mail a letter according to zip code.

With much less reason or impetus, we as a people are constantly forming clubs, associations, groups, and societies; so, of course, there are now several organized anti-the-numbers-racket groups, including the Anti-Digit Dialing League of San Francisco and Washington, D.C.'s, Committee of Ten Million to Oppose All-Number Calling.

At the risk of attracting lightning bolts from this organized, aroused citizenry, I would like to say a word in defense of the new telephone numbers. I find it most convenient, when calling farther than across the street, to be connected with my party after completing the dialing in less time than it took to do the dialing. Sure, in many ways I miss the usually cheerful tones of the telephone operator, but believe me, I don't miss spending ten minutes trying to pronounce phonetically and then spelling "Peapack," when trying to reach home from Boston, Chicago, Florida, or California.

" 'P' as in Peter, 'E' as in egg, 'A' as in apple, 'pack' as in pistol pack—no, not pistolpack. Peapack as in peapod. No! Not peapodpack. *Peapack*"—and so forth! I have spent in all, I am sure, a measurable percentage of my life spelling it out for sometimes incredulous operators. Now all I need to do is dial ten numbers, and I have never yet had an argument with the electronic gear that translates my dialing into the happy tones of my wife's voice at the other end.

I am such a hopeless square that I think this new system really *is* progress.

11/15/63

Although it is often said that nothing sounds sweeter to a person than his own name, it looks like this music will be heard less and less.

The computer, along with all its other wondrous accomplishments, has reduced us all to digits.

And therein lies a danger great and real.

Do *you* know what one or more Washington, D.C., master computers say of you? For that matter, do you know what the local one says of your credit? Says about your character or lack of it?

Computer data banks aren't collecting data for no purpose and no profit. Like any business or bank, they sell what they contain for use and at a profit or for a purpose.

One of the more memorable times of the many times that my wife has had occasion to be irked with her husband occurred on one of her very rare safaris into New York City to do some shopping at Bloomingdale's. Being a Scotsman who hates to part with actual folding money, I suggested she use our Bloomingdale's credit card. She'd no sooner completed her sale-priced purchases and produced the credit card than she found herself being politely but firmly escorted upstairs to the credit department. There, a sour-faced matron literally grabbed the card from her hand, took a scissors, and cut it in half, observing that they had been looking for it, and her, for some time.

Now my bride of twenty-five years is quite shy, quite retiring—but I want you to know that her telephone call to me from Bloomingdale's credit department reflected none of her normal restraints.

It developed that months earlier a few of some things purchased had arrived broken and had been returned for credit. The computer didn't get the word and month after month had been flashing us up as dangerous mountebanks running amuck with a creditless Bloomingdale's credit card.

I cite and oversimplify this tale, not because it's unique, but because practically everyone can top this computer story with a worse experience of his own.

There is just no way in the days and decades to come that our digits won't increasingly dominate our lives. Our numbers, not our names, now and for the rest of our days on earth are what will matter.

So if simple justice is to prevail in this land of cherished individuality and individual rights, computer input and output must be as subject to law, regulation, control as anything or anyone else. Computer feeders must be subject to vigorous scrutiny, held vigorously to account for wrong as well as error.

Today, thank heavens, Congress is working at the problem. Congressman Koch of New York City and Senator Bayh of Indiana have measures in the hopper that would make every government computer-keeping agency tell any citizen on whom they're keeping a record that the record is there; provide him with a print-out so that he may correct errors, refute refutable statements, and forbid the passing on of such data without the citizen's permission.

That's the sort of thing, the sort of direction, the sort of law that must be enacted on multiple levels before our individual freedoms are strangled by digits in data banks.

4/15/71

Congress for some time has been considering new legislation more effectively prohibiting and/or rigorously controlling wiretapping and its wireless electronic age improvements. So have a number of states.

It's long past time that such legislation was legislated, complete with sharp, effective teeth.

Just as the right to be heard is essential to a meaningful democracy governing free people, equally vital is the right to be *unheard*, the right to privacy . . . the old hallowed Englishism "A man's home is his castle."

The Orwellian Big-Brother-is-watching-you nightmare is now not fiction, but fact.

The Eye is no longer just that of the government, legal probers and enforcers, and CIA spies; it isn't just husbands and wives trying to get or avoid alimony. The Eye blinks for some corporations in competitors' laboratories and at competitors' sales strategy meetings. Or for insurance companies who suspect fraud. In fact, for all manner of people for all manner of reasons.

There should really be no basic difficulty for reasonable men in Congress to get the job done. It needn't be hung up by disagreement between those who would totally prohibit the invasion of privacy and those who would permit it with safeguards in certain areas of law enforcement.

Under careful court surveillance involving more than one judge and at a high level, permission could be extended in areas of the most heinous crimes, as well as of course in areas *really* pertaining to national security.

All the rest of it, by any device whatsoever, can be done away with in a relatively simple manner.

By providing both heavy fines and/or jail sentences for anyone who engages in the invasion of privacy, it would make the potential risk not worth taking, the results too self-convicting to be of value.

As has oft and truly been said, eternal vigilance is the price of liberty. Big Brothers inside the borders are just as menacing to our freedom—and much more pernicious—than the readily identifiable ideological enemies outside our borders.

12/15/67

What in heaven's name is per se criminal about gambling?

What's the crime against person or state if man (down,

Lib girls—in this sense "man" includes you too) wants to wager on a race of any sort, on the chance a number may turn up, on the outcome of a game, or on where the bouncing ball finally stops?

Making criminal this thing is unmeasurably costly. It provides the greatest source of corruption of law enforcers and lawmakers. And it does more to cause people to lose respect for law itself than most anything else.

Imagine if the police and law enforcement officials of cities, counties, states, and the federal government didn't have to spend vast amounts of time and money trying to enforce unenforceable laws against wagering, and could devote that time and that money to waging war against actual crime and criminals.

It's criminal, this present situation.

Now that every company and every level of government is struggling to reorder priorities in the face of more demands than there is money, it's the right time to reorder the priorities of police and law enforcers. Let 'em focus on truly criminal areas—such as the trafficking of hard drugs.

7/15/71

Today, eighteen years after the end of World War II, we have more than a quarter of a million American troops in Europe. Maintaining them there is hugely expensive. It contributes most measurably to our gold imbalance.

Is the presence of American forces in this huge number still necessary? This question is being raised with increasing frequency, not only by those concerned with spending, but also by some dealing with defense and the affairs of state. The critical gold problem, of course, has precipitated much of the current debate. But before looking at that aspect, consider some of the military angles.

The past decade has seen the development of a vast jet transport fleet. In hours our forces can be deployed in very large numbers anywhere on the globe with adequate landing fields. They can certainly be returned to present European posts from bases in this country overnight. Additionally, in contrast to the postwar years, our NATO Allies are now prosperous and can afford a more substantial share of their own defense.

Is it, from a military-deterrent point of view, still essential, as it was ten years ago, to keep so many American troops in Europe? Is a reduction of the number involved possible under the changed circumstances?

It seems to me that is a valid question regardless of our international monetary problem. But, of course, we cannot view it without considering that problem because it is a critical one. The nibbling measures of the Administration have had little or no impact on our growing gold deficit. There is a most serious question as to the effectiveness or soundness of the present Administration proposals to discriminate against the purchase of foreign securities by Americans. Our forces abroad and our military aid to Allies account for a sizable slice of the deficit pie. It is obvious that a reduction in their number would mean a proportionate reduction in that deficit.

There is a psychological effect to consider, too. A reduction in our forces in Europe might stimulate our Allies to shoulder a bit more of the expense of their own defense.

It is generally conceded that in the event of an all-out "conventional" land assault by Russia, she could soon reach the English Channel. It is not the number of American forces present which is the prime deterrent. It is the American presence at the borders of the Iron Curtain on the seas of the Mediterranean and our unadulterated commitment via NATO to meet and return any assault on the free nations of

Western Europe. In view of the situation today, cannot the President, the Secretary of Defense, and the Secretary of State re-examine the question of the size of American forces maintained abroad?

10/1/63

It's always startling when smart people do something obviously stupid.

The fantastic accomplishments of the indefatigable Japanese in penetrating and frequently dominating the marketplaces for the manufactured goods of this world is the stuff of which legends are made. Their GNP exceeds that of every power in the world except ours and West Germany's.

In major measure, though, Japan's whole prosperity, growth, future depend on continued acceptance in these markets of other lands. With protectionism running stronger throughout the world than it has been since the early twenties, you'd think the Japanese, with their extraordinary sensitivity, would be striving to stem such a tide.

Instead, they seem to be doing quite the contrary. They continue to shut competitors out of their markets. They sometimes apparently "dump" subsidized goods in the other fellow's home front, and otherwise proceed oblivious to the present inflammable condition of world trade.

Surely, somebody can get through to responsible Tokyo ears and advise them Japan has a growing world problem. They have achieved so extraordinarily, it would be a shame to see the Japanese set back for almost completely unnecessary, avoidable, voidable reasons.

6/15/71

Disturbed as I was to hear Senator Goldwater promise to end the draft if elected, I found it even more upsetting to have the Defense Department rushing into print with the statement that "We are glad to know the Republican candidate agrees with the Administration that the draft should be ended as soon as possible." Right now the Senator from Arizona has no real responsibility in the matter, but the Administration, and particularly the Department of Defense, most certainly does.

If anyone should know that we cannot maintain an armed force totaling 2.7 million men on a purely voluntary basis, the Pentagon braid should. As for those civilians who head up the Defense Department and speak for it on policy matters—well, if they are prepared to double the pay scales, halve the military workweek, recommend overtime and time and a half for Saturday and Sunday for those in uniform, and increase retirement provisions, then indeed they might get along with a totally voluntary service with quotas filled and perhaps even a waiting list.

Under the present circumstances, however, to suggest we can meet our responsibilities and maintain needed military manpower without a draft is shockingly irresponsible at best or a most inappropriate, crummy bit of political palaver from the one section of the federal government that ought to be most removed from election-time partisanship.

If some nuts in the Defense Department have such thoughts, they need only study the lands that have tried it— including most recently our British cousins and our Canadian neighbors.

In a purely voluntary service you get two types for the most part—the best and the worst.

Fortunately, the greatest percentage of career men in the officer echelon and among all ranks are those motivated by a combination of such things as the particular appeal of the service or branch, the responsibilities involved, patriotism, a daily knowledge of the essentialness of their work, the unique camaraderie of career servicemen.

At the opposite end of the scale are many of those thinking of escape from empty or unhappy civilian circumstances, those to whom no other job is open, etc.

In between is the great bulk of men who are in the navy or the air force or the marine corps initially because of the reasonable expectation of being drafted sooner or later into the army. To get the service they prefer, they volunteer. With no draft such enlistments would disappear.

It is certainly reasonable to study present draft procedures to see if all the assorted grounds for deferment are equitable or not, to see if some method could be found for having the obligation come up for disposal one way or another at a certain age or stage, to find within affordable bounds means of upping pay scales tied to length of service as well as rank and skill, etc.

Compulsory service or the lack of it will have very little effect on the cream of the military crop, those who have chosen a career in the armed forces. To imagine that officer ranks fed from ROTC and full-college-scholarship pools could be maintained when there was no draft looming at any stage in a young man's life is unrealistic. To think that the hundreds of thousands in enlisted ranks would ever volunteer or stay in with no draft in the background is just plain silly.

Talk of study and revision is fair enough and, indeed, most sensible.

To make it sound like the Administration was about to do away with the draft just to blunt the appeal of Senator Goldwater's campaign promise is worse than foolish. It is not honest.

10/15/64

By midyear President Nixon has promised an end to the draft. He has also made it clear that our armed forces will remain strong, that is, large in number—an estimated 2 million.

The young are not the only ones who fervently hope these twin objectives are accomplishable rather than contradictory. Usually, I'm not a pessimistic man, but I think the likelihood of being able to maintain enough competent warm bodies of combat-capable troops on a volunteer basis is a bit unlikely.

This country's seventeeners and eighteeners don't seem to get sent as readily by 6:00 A.M. trumpets and leather-lunged sergeants as they do by Led Zeppelins, Jefferson Airplanes, Rolling Stones, and the non-Churchillian Blood, Sweat, and Tears.

True, pay scales now for service in the Services are generally higher than many jobs available to inexperienced youngsters in civilian life. True, fringe benefits are substantial. True, retirement comes sooner than one might think and at a better rate than one could expect from most other professions.

But, you see, at seventeen and eighteen these things all seem a long way down a very long road. By the time you have traversed that road and look back, you're a bit too old in body and soul and mind to be what the services have in mind when they refer to combat-ready capability.

The technical jobs and the desk jobs and the good jobs can probably be met from the ranks of volunteers. And maybe we'll all get the surprise of our lives by finding out there are enough tens of thousands of youngsters who for a variety of reasons—and there *are* many good ones—will fill the multiple slots every year.

I repeat, though, it'll come as one big surprise if it turns out to be so.

1/1/73

On the subject of the young, their views and their education, I was happy to learn that Latin is less and less of a must these days in schools and for college admission.

As one who struggled painfully (it took me 3½ years to pass second-year Caesar), I found it hard either to encourage or admonish most of my own young, who have gone through the same difficulty.

Surely, today there are a million other more relevant disciplines to educate, broaden the mind of young people. A man can use, understand, and enjoy language and languages without necessarily knowing the far-back roots of same—just as you can know and enjoy a tree or a forest without being a root specialist.

Latin died once, and I am glad to know that it is doing so again.

7/15/69

Trees sent Joyce Kilmer, but nothing quite sends most Americans like the smell of a new car interior and the soul-satisfying sound of shutting a new car door.

There are few among us who don't find that sound as exciting as any bar of music. There are few among us who do not put a new chariot's aroma on a par with the perfume of the loveliest blooms.

It's a deep yearning for both of these that, at this time of year, drives so many to the nearest automobile showroom.

Call it what you want, or call for the psychiatrist, but it's a powerful fact of American life.

5/15/67

A TRAVELER'S SIMILES

As rare as an English waiter in London.
As rare as cordiality in France.

As rare as a good bullfight in Spain.
As rare as a haggleless price in Morocco.
As rare as good spaghetti in Rome.
As rare as an unkind Italian.
As rare as a music hater in Austria.
As rare as a reasonable price in Germany.
As rare as an unpleasant Dane.

9/1/70

As a lusty gust turned my umbrella inside out the other evening, I suddenly realized that the biggest thing umbrella makers have going for them is not rain.

It's wind.

6/15/72

How do you suppose Senator McGovern must now feel when it turns out his "miracle" nomination seems to have been a CREEPY accomplishment?

6/15/73

Practicing
What You Preach

How to end unemployment and ensure renewed prosperity for many years to come:
Institute the four-day workweek.

5/1/71

Most Forbes, Inc. employees have been on the four-day work-week for several months. They love it, and from management's point of view, the pluses way outweigh any minuses.

But, I am told, one surprising source of complaint has cropped up—for various and imaginable reasons, it turns out that a number of wives don't like their husbands home that much.

4/15/72

FOUR-DAY WORKWEEK

A hot, good thing for a presidential aspirant to be for.

I wonder why none so far has spoken of it.

Who do you think will be sharp enough to be first?

3/15/72

Just a year ago, primarily at my instigation, *Forbes* instituted the four-day workweek.

No one likes to confess failure. For us, after a year's wholehearted go at it, in too many respects from a management's viewpoint, it has proved unsuccessful.

I don't think one can generalize from our failure, because *Forbes* is essentially a service business with press deadlines and small departments where there had to be skeleton crews on Friday.

At first we had some advantages. *Forbes'* workweek was thirty-five hours to begin with, so we simply lengthened the four workdays so there was no loss of actual hours. We reasoned that there would be more efficient output during the longer working days, that there would be a reduction of absenteeism. There was.

I also felt strongly that the wave of the future was—is— in this direction, that many of the best of the younger generation have a burning determination to have time to do the things they want to do (in addition to working for a living) while they are young enough to do them—travel, sports, games, hobbies, and just togetherness or, as they would put it, time to Get It All Together.

I still do not think these reasons are invalid.

But the four-day workweek's undoing for us was simply that too often it became a three-day workweek in terms of fully manned departments. Friday's covering force was off on Monday. Supervisors were off on one or the other, and that had its effect on work flow.

Of course, when there was a major holiday, a number of people felt gypped if it came on their three-day weekend and they didn't get another day off. If it came midweek, the workweek literally was three days. When people occasionally had to work on the fifth day because of illness or vacation or absences, they felt entitled to equivalent days off later.

And our costs for temporary help have soared. When you must get work done in four days and do not carry an excess number of employees, you must fill in with temps during vacations, illnesses, absences.

At the beginning there was some employee unhappiness about the necessity of getting to work earlier and not being able to go home until later. This wore off, though, as people became accustomed and grew to like the three-day weekends. At their request the one-hour lunch hour was reduced to forty-five minutes so they could leave one-fourth of an hour earlier in the evening. These problems and adjustments coming on-stream to the four-day workweek, however, didn't present major problems.

I guess the principal problem comes from the relative smallness in numbers of our departments and the necessity for all of them to be manned, to one degree or another, five days a week.

One day, when and if the majority of businesses are on a four-day week, we'll find a way to go back to it for as many people as possible.

That day isn't here. We have a business—a service business—to run and customers to satisfy. After a year's try at doing it in four days, we just weren't getting the job done as thoroughly and as well as we wanted to. It's a disappointment to us all. But to stay in business, any business, one must recognize a mistake when it's made—no matter how well intended.

10/15/72

Politics

This writer is running in New Jersey's April primary for the Republican nomination as state senator from Somerset County. It is in response to an overwhelming demand—on my part. Some people bowl, play golf, play cards, or garden as a hobby; others build models, or collect stamps when not working at their job. I just happen to be fascinated by government, by politics and have studied it and followed it from childhood. There is no halo around this head that prompted me months ago to start campaigning for this particular nomination.

But isn't it amazing that so few men in business enter public life? Today laws, rules, regulations affect us all from the beginning of our lives until long after death, when our estate is settled. Increasingly, every phase of business is under regulation by government; every one of our freedoms is subject to the laws of men in public office; our destiny as individuals and as a nation is in the hands of a handful of elected officials. Yet, knowing all this, few men in any community are willing to run for office. Sometimes they vote, but more times they simply complain about the People in office. Today most people call a man a politician when they are trying to use a polite term to indicate they think he's either a crook, a liar, a renegade, or all those things put together. It's like calling a man a capitalist—he's supposed to deny the charge, or resent the use of such a "dirty word."

Why don't more trained, able men run for public office when they know how great is the power of elected officials to determine how our lives shall be run? Many are the excuses:

"I'm too busy" or "haven't time" or "it would interfere with my business." You might have more time for business, and longer to live if you sent fewer incompetents to Washington. Their laws can ruin your business, and complying with them can take all your spare time.

"I'll be glad to serve if no one runs against me and I don't have to campaign." What a nervy stipulation! Don't you have competition at your job? At school? In your charitable fund-raising drives? At the card game? On the golf course? Why not for something as vital to all people as public office? Campaigning takes time, but surely it is time well spent if you help get better men in office. It is as much as a civic contribution to provide voters with a choice of candidates as it is to help in the Red Cross.

"Politics is so dirty; I can't stand mudslinging." Of course, in politics there are dirty tactics and clean tactics—just as in business. Of course, there's mudslinging, and one's personal life is under the microscope—but it can never match the choice personal gossip around a bridge table, or the remarks you make about some of your business competitors. Why expect politics to be any different?

"Politics is so corrupt." There are crooks in politics, maybe more than there should be. But there are crooks in business and in the professions. It is no monopoly. And a politician can't be corrupt by himself—someone has to corrupt him. As often as not, it is some esteemed citizen, such as yourself, who likes to get a traffic ticket killed or phone a big political wheel for a "favorable ruling" about some irritating regulation. Politics, like business and life itself, is what you as a voter make it.

I'm running because I like it, but more men better start running for office, because it's important—a far more important contribution to our welfare than any other worthwhile community activity.

2/15/51

THE WHITE HOUSE
WASHINGTON

August 19, 1957

Dear Senator Forbes:

As your friends join in greeting you on this anniversary, it is a pleasure to be counted among them. And naturally our thoughts are centered upon wishing you many happy returns

of the day, with the next one finding you in the Governor's chair.
    With warm regard,

                                    Sincerely,
                            Dwight D. Eisenhower

The Honorable Malcolm Forbes
Far Hills
New Jersey

The other day one of our sons brought in the above
letter from the *Forbes* collection of Presidential Letters.
"Pop, in a few days you'll be fifty-one. Do you remember
what happened this time thirteen years ago?"

For me the fiery political flames were banked and died
over a decade ago. But I remember feeling like such a hypo-
crite when people would say, during the course of my numerous political campaigns in the years immediately following
World War II, how much they admired any young man
devoting so much time to public life. Fired throughout youth
by vaulting political ambition, nothing could then have kept
me from politics.

Now nothing could induce me to undertake *any* political
post, and I have come genuinely to admire and appreciate
good men who do. It really does mean, you know, giving up
virtually all prospects of earning much money, all chance of
occasional carefree quiet.

Instead of just one boss in the office and one at home,
men questing and/or having public office have a thousand
thousand bosses: everyone who votes or will grow to vote,
every Interest, every pressure group, every ethnic group.
Every individual mad about anything trivial or momentous
feels free and is free to have his demands heard and sometimes heeded by publicos.

How my wife hated the whole business. The business

of touring and waving and sitting on platforms and accepting flowers and being called on for a few words she found infinitely more painful than bearing our babies. And I believe, with a few notable exceptions, that this is true of most wives of political figures, including every first lady except perhaps Dolly Madison and Mrs. Franklin D. Roosevelt.

What's all this got to do with business and the economy and the stock market and next-quarter earnings and who's running what companies how well?

Nothing really, except birthdays remind even businessmen, able and young and old and able, that age we must and age we do and at a rate that sometimes seems very, very fast.

The man who said *tempus fugit* was wrong.

It goes like lightning.

Tomorrow does come and we're all very soon gone.

So, in living, let live—when you've anything to say about the matter.

8/15/70

Often officeholders/seekers begin their speeches with the observation that they stand in front of their audience "in deep humility."

By the time the speech is finished they—and the audience—are usually deep in something else.

8/1/72

Alcohol and aspirin.

One is associated with merriment and happy high times of mind and occasion.

The other is associated with nothing but headaches and most every other ache known to man (and Ms.).

Thus by these definitions in terms of association, the former should be considered Good, and the latter Bad.

So if you never knew what "specious reasoning" is, now you do.

Keep it in mind when you hear and read millions of words by thousands of candidates.

10/15/72

Along with mothers-in-law, congressmen are America's favorite whipping boys. As the current session pushes toward adjournment, the usual chorus of gripes against congressmen rises from a thousand typewriters and a thousand rostrums.

At the risk of being shot at as un-American during this open season on our lawmakers, I'd like to defend the much-maligned congressmen. Yes, all of them. Even that handful who are so benighted and willful as to fail to see things my way.

I'll defend, for example, the mail weighers. This group, much scorned by high-minded do-gooders, actually performs a rather useful function in our society. The mailwatchers, those sensitive souls, have but one conviction: the importance of their own reelection. About burning issues, expect no firm expressions of opinions from them. To do may be to die if they decide to reason why on a legislative hot potato. They weigh, not the issue, but the mail.

Perhaps this type of congressman is not exactly a social scientist's idea of what the Founding Fathers had in mind for Congress. But the stubborn fact is that they perform a valuable function all the same. No scientist has yet devised a seismograph more sensitive than a congressman holding up a wet finger into the political winds. No rhapsodic rhetoric about ideals or visions of sugar plums will garner their vote— unless it looks like most of the "folks back home" have been moved too—and first. In short, the mail watcher, however timid his character, plays a rather important part in making representative government really representative.

In further defense of our legislative branch, I'd like to mention an even larger group. This sizable majority of representatives spends month after month trying to figure out what *they* think may be best for the country by the way of a new law or no new law. These misguided fellows aren't obliging enough to accept my opinion—sometimes not even yours. They've even indicated our personal opinion may be selfishly motivated, that there may be two sides to the issue. These fellows may even listen to those who disagree with us.

So they go on and do all sorts of foolish things for a good many hours after any sensible man has gone home from work. They hold committee hearings, public and private. They pass hours listening to visiting constituents. They even seem to spend a lot of time answering their mail and looking into, firsthand, some of the operations of government for which the committees they belong to are responsible.

Taking into account all three categories of congressmen —the stubborn, the seismographers, and the bunch we were just talking about—it is sort of a wonder anything good gets done by them. Yet it does. That's why I wanted to take time out from the good old American sport of congressmen-sniping to say a word on behalf of our lawmakers.

9/1/61

It's getting to be the time of year when some members of many assorted congressional committees travel abroad to see at first hand what the Congress hath wrought.

As inevitable as these congressional travels is the rash of annual editorials which will deplore these junkets and their cost.

Forbes would like to lodge a minority opinion.

We think such field trips by senators and congressmen are overwhelmingly valuable. Scenes and people, countries and governments seen firsthand are infinitely more valuable for the forming of opinion and judgment than most compilations served up in printed form at committee hearings.

Sure, an occasional Capitol Hiller sounds off in a stupid or insulting fashion in some land he is visiting and complicates life for the State Department.

This danger, and the cost of congressional travel, is, however, very heavily offset by the great pluses of having those who legislate on our relations abroad getting as much firsthand knowledge as possible.

7/15/65

Regulatory agencies, particularly the federal ones, are often considered the *bête noire* of the regulated—especially business. Damning the regulators is such a habit that even the regulated who occasionally dominate the regulators continue to down 'em.

The thoughtful businessman, though, knows very well in his heart and head that regulatory agencies which do what they are supposed to do provide prime insurance for relatively free enterprise's survival.

Left nearly alone at the turn of the century, the robber barons of steel, oil, tobacco, railroads, meat-packing, and the like showed such naked avaricious monopoly power and public-be-damnedness that it took all the clout of that day's courageous press (then known as muckrakers) plus the dynamic Teddy Roosevelt to slow them down.

Still relatively unregulated, business so blew it in the twenties that the ensuing Depression very nearly resulted in business being put out of business. Only damned-by-business Franklin D. Roosevelt saved free enterprise, by government spending and a spate of alphabetized new regulatory federal agencies.

I was reminded of all this when I happened to read the label on a favorite patent medicine the other day. Do you suppose for one minute that its admonitions, ingredients, and plain words would be there if the Food and Drug Administration wasn't?

Sure, some regulatory agencies need knocking from time to time—like the Federal Power Commission, which seems more concerned with regulating short-term rates than spurring crisis steps to meet a dire and swiftly accelerating power shortage.

Let's face it—federal regulations keep more companies honest than, honestly, would be otherwise.

Yes, some regulatory agencies need knocking—but more for what they don't do by way of their jobs than what they do when they fully do their jobs.

9/15/72

There's only one merit to all the bull being written by those who claim the assassination of President Kennedy was a complicated plot involving several people and at least a couple of other gunmen: Spinning these fantasies provides a living for the writers, headlines for Garrison-ilk politicos, and hypos the newsstand sales of magazines.

One of the current paperbacks in the flood on the subject is entitled *Whitewash*.

They all could be entitled more descriptively—*Hogwash*.

1/1/68

The shocking shooting of Governor Wallace has once again unleashed a torrent of stuff and guff about ours being a nation of violence. Personally, I think 99 percent of all this psychoanalytical verbiage is completely wide of the mark.

Almost no long-civilized country permits the possession by private citizens of weapons. Possessing one is a crime of high order. In this country virtually anyone's entitled to go a-gunning.

Efforts to curb indiscriminate gun owning by Americans that followed previous spectacular political assassinations have been thwarted because the members of United States firearms associations have an incredible lobbying capability. They're good people who feel the right to bear private arms is part of the American heritage—that it is a personal assurance of freedom as well as a sporting necessity comparable to fishing rods. Their response to any gun-limiting proposals exceeds that of insurance-claims lawyers on no-fault insurance proposals.

Maybe—it's a mighty small maybe—we could get legislation at least making it a major crime for any but law enforcement officers to possess handguns, since these are the means of most of our fifty-seven daily firearms deaths. Despite the rifle killings of John Kennedy, Martin Luther King, rifles play a far less lethal part in our hundreds and hundreds of annual bullet murders.

I don't think we are one whit worse or better or different from the British or the French or the Italians or the Spaniards or the Japanese or the Australians or the Scandinavians or the Russians or the Chinese or the Indians or any other people when it comes to violence. We differ only in that we let nearly everybody and anybody have the gun means to make their tempers and temperaments lethal.

It's surely time for sportsmen to help curb gunmen instead of being inadvertent fronts for 'em.

6/15/72

To read extracts from the diary of the young man who nearly succeeded in assassinating Governor Wallace is a quite terrifying, chilling thing. He made six tries to get President Nixon, considered Senator McGovern, and settled for an opportunity at Wallace.

He wrote of his failure on the President's life in Canada, "I had a good view as he came by me again—the sixth time and still alive. . . . Should go to Washington. Can't kill Nixie boy if you ain't close to him. . . .

"Yesterday I even considered McGovern as a target. . . .

"Make the First Lady a widow . . . how to do a bang-up job of getting people to notice you. . . .

". . . I decided Wallace would have the honor, or what would you call it?"

Despite the comprehensiveness of security for the President of the United States, Lincoln and Garfield and McKinley and Kennedy were killed on the job, and shooting attempts were made on Roosevelt and Truman. If it is so difficult to make Presidents safe, the job of safeguarding primary presidential candidates would seem nearly impossible if a fanatic sets out to get them.

I guess no one has the answer to protecting those who are less than Presidents, since we don't even have the answer to saving the chief executive. But, surely, can we not insist that at least the two presidential candidates campaign more safely (and, not incidentally, more sanely) by a greater use of television studios to talk to people and less use of public rallies and parades and handshaking?

If men have the sense to be President, and are the selection of their party for the race, isn't it about time that they cooperate and collaborate in safeguarding their lives? This certainly would show more respect for the responsibility they bear to those who pick them.

Democracy cannot be operative when bullets have as much to do with determining the winner as ballots. I think we are at the point of maturity in this country where people would admire a man's guts if he didn't unnecessarily risk spilling them.

10/1/72

As one of many thousands who attended the GOP Convention, I came away fortified in the conviction that the present method of nominating candidates for President and Vice-President is outmoded and should be junked.

I believe the voters of a party should name the nominee. Under the present setup, it is incredibly difficult to make their views prevail. The convention system makes it easy for the bosses and "the deals" to operate, although often, as in the Republican instance, they have been turned back in the end. The only answer, despite certain shortcomings, is a national primary to name the candidates. The cost? It could hardly exceed what was spent by the two leading candidates in the various primaries and preconvention campaigning. The method? By a system somewhat similar to the present November election. The value? A majority of the people themselves name their men. There can be no argument as to who "wuz robbed."

The convention system served its purpose in the days before press wire services, radio, and TV made it possible for all to form opinions on candidates and their views. Today it is a clumsy, largely undemocratic, and expensive anachronism. We should throw it out and provide by federal law for a national primary.

8/1/52

State presidential primaries—their usefulness this year is in demonstrating their uselessness.

As he frequently is, Senate Democratic Leader Mike Mansfield is right on with his proposed constitutional amendment which would establish a national presidential primary election.

In past years, when there was just a handful of states with primaries of long standing, it was fun and games for everybody except the losers. Now, with everybody getting into the act, the states' presidential primaries are really costly Roman circuses, with estimable men savagely clawing each other in local arenas where pressing, often local, issues have to be embraced, frequently at the price of principle.

Mansfield's amendment is being cosponsored by that sagacious Republican dean, Vermont's George Aiken. It provides for a primary early in August of presidential years with the party nomination going to the candidate polling the most votes, as long as the total is at least 40 percent of the votes cast. If no one receives 40 percent, the top two have a runoff four weeks later. The parties would still hold the traditional convention to name a Vice-President and adopt a platform.

This proposed amendment makes so much sense that I suppose it will be a long time happening.

4/15/72

Wipe out college.

The Electoral College, that is.

It's not merely that the constitutional provisions for it are anachronistic, but its continued existence is downright dangerous to our democratic system.

It's not merely that Presidents can be and have been elected who have lost the popular vote, but its existence forces presidential candidates to emphasize issues important in critical states but not necessarily of national significance. The Electoral College also makes the barnstorming, handshaking stuff and nonsense seem necessary to help carry states where the race seems close.

From all I've read, studied, and thought about the matter I can't find one good reason why the President and Vice-President shouldn't be elected by popular vote.

There are, of course, a number of purely political reasons why many state machines and their machinators like the present system. It gives them an influence on presidential candidates that they should not have.

So long as the Electoral College votes of every state are determined by the merest majority, it is essential for a national candidate to truckle to the Daleys and other dillys, to special interests and pressure pockets whose concern for the national weal is quite often quite secondary.

There are many people who feel Mr. Nixon is more politician than statesman. If, pronto, he could put into the works a constitutional amendment to let the American people in the future directly elect the President, he would quickly establish that his concern is for the whole country, and that the necessarily narrower interests of local politicos are not going to unduly deter his determination to do what's best, what's right.

It's a tough one to start out on, because the opposition will be politically bipartisan and powerful, but the people will support the new President in seeking this change.

One shudders to think how bitterly rent, how horrendously divided and confused the United States would be at this moment if the election of a President were still not decided, still up for grabs in the House.

12/1/68

I cannot conceive of a worse way than determining by elections who shall be state and local judges. In New York State, as well as thirty-eight others, even supreme court justices are elected, and most run again after six to ten years.

From limited personal experience and limitless observation, I am as aware as surely everyone else must be of the pressures and obligations that are involved in winning (or losing, for that matter) public office. Wheeling and dealing and paying and collecting and truth and hypocrisy and evasion and squaring circles are the day-in and day-out routine of those who would be mayors and councilmen and aldermen and assemblymen and state legislators and congressmen and governors and Presidents. From that crucible we get more good men than bad, but as proving ground for judges, it's about as relevant as how many pie-eating contests they've won.

A judge should not owe his judgeship to his ability to machinate with bosses and protesters, minorities and majorities, paid campaign workers, or the unpaid ambitious. His robes and his bench should not be at the beck or the recall of voters aroused by the positions taken by one party or the other on Vietnam, welfare, unemployment, or the like.

The system whereby Presidents, governors, top elected officials appoint judges subject to approval by the upper legislative body has proved for a long time to be, over all, the wisest way to fill the bench.

Sure, there are some politics involved—acquaintance with, or at least avoiding the ire of, one's federal or state senator; often a record of party participation; and, best of all from the viewpoint of the job seeker, friendship with the appointing executive or his closest aides.

But governors as well as Presidents have long come to know that they gain more by prestigious appointments to the bench than by choosing hacks who hack it up where justice and a knowledge of law are required.

The sooner those still electing judges stop doing so, the better for all concerned.

10/1/72

By the time Dwight Eisenhower left Washington, some 69 percent of the ambassadors he had named were career men, one of the highest percentages in the country's recent history. Ike's emphasis on picking so-called professionals was widely lauded, of course, in U.S. Foreign Service circles. In general, it had the approval of the public. At a recent count about 63 percent of the ambassadors named by President Kennedy were from the career Foreign Service. In other words, there has been a small increase in the percentage of so-called political appointments. This has been criticized in some quarters in Washington and around the country.

I think the critics are wrong. I think selecting as ambassadors only career Foreign Service men is a mistake. The policy has been far overdone. Sure, at first blush it seems to make sense to have the United States represented in a foreign country by a man who, through training and experience, knows well the operations of the Foreign Service and the State Department. Such men know the procedures, the routines, and the protocol. Usually—but by no means always—they have had previous exposure on lower echelons in the country to which they are named.

But on reflection, don't these very assets often serve also as limitations? An ambassador is properly responsible for every aspect of his country and his countrymen's activities in a foreign land. He is the person of the United States. His judgments, his recommendations, his perceptions, his foresight, his imagination, all can play a vital part in our relations with the country concerned. A career man by definition tends to move within the often limiting atmosphere and cliques of his own service bureaucracy. His livelihood, his career, his future, totally depend on how his performance is rated by his Foreign Service superiors in Washington.

On the other hand, the oft-sneered-at "political" ambassador has given no such hostage to fortune. He is not under the same pressure to limit his observations or recommendations to those which might be better liked on the home front. Usually, noncareer ambassadors are men of great accomplishment and prestige in other fields: education, business, law, other branches of government, and politics. Their appointments often spring, of course, from their activities on behalf of the party in power. Occasionally, it is true, they prove blunderers or duds as ambassadors. But this hazard is not limited to the outsiders. Career men have on occasion proven less than successful in the top spots.

The gradual change to a higher proportion of career men has been valuable. A Bohlen in Moscow was of infinitely greater value to the United States than a Joe Davies. So, too, with men such as Llewellyn Thompson and Robert Murphy. But who can deny that this nation has benefited from a Dwight Morrow in Mexico, a John Sherman Cooper in India, an Edwin Reischauer in Japan. All were political appointments.

A couple of years ago the head of a foreign government said to me in the course of an off-the-record conversation: "Your Ambassador is an able man, a nice man, but he is a career man. He wouldn't dream of taking up our problems and requests and complaints with the Secretary of State or the President. Career men go through channels and never get to the top. I wish our country was considered big enough and important enough to get an American appointed as ambassador who was a personal friend of the Secretary of State or the President. Then we know our views wouldn't be buried in the files of a State Department desk downstairs."

Logical from their point of view, and not without merit from ours.

The premise that a career ambassador is ipso facto a good appointment and that a political appointment is ipso facto bad is just plain silly.

10/15/62

Cabinet members who seek to establish a following or a base or a policy independent of the President simply don't understand what their job is. This President and every President deserves and should either demand the full loyalty of his Cabinet members or can the recalcitrant. Unlike the President and elected officials, Cabinet members have a constituency of one—the President. Their mission is to serve him or else depart—*gracefully*.

12/15/70

Has it ever occurred to you, if we had not adopted the limit of two terms for the President of the United States, who would still be the President of the United States?

Dwight D. Eisenhower.

3/1/68

Christmas Thoughts

Books have been written on the subject of graffiti with pseudo-serious commentary and much quotation.

Here's one for someone's next compilation—reported by our London operative as seen among the obscenities on the walls of an underground lavatory last December:

"Holiday greetings to all our readers."

12/15/71

Have you ever heard Dylan Thomas' recording of his essay *A Child's Christmas in Wales?*

If not, you should. I know nothing which so movingly evokes the spirit of this season and the day. I was tempted to print copious extracts as *Forbes'* Christmas editorial, but resisted because so much more of the words' meaning is conveyed by the voice of this troubled, inspired Welshman who died tragically young.

So many at this time of year bewail the commercialization of Christmas, fearing that the raison d'être of Christmas is buried by tons of tinsel and tinkle. I don't at all share that lament.

In Christ's time and before it and since, decoration and celebration have been man's way of marking occasions and reflecting joy. That the occasion of the greatest joy in the Christian world should occasion the longest and greatest celebrations and decorations is highly fitting indeed.

Perhaps it's wrong that it's so, but I think some of the spirit of Christmas would suffer if the merchants did not gaily and brightly decorate their stores and the streets, if the airwaves didn't reverberate with old hymns and new jingles. What's wrong with selling the gifts that people want to give and be given? For virtually everyone there is as much joy and often more in buying for family and friends as in receiving from them. If my memory doesn't fault me, that spirit is one of the things Christ came to teach.

If one cannot be happy during this season without some devils to damn, try a new approach—instead of the merchants, let's damn the devil He talked of, who still happens to be around and in us all.

12/15/63

A year ago on Christmas Eve in Akron, Ohio, a couple walked up to the registration desk of the downtown Holiday Inn, followed by a donkey.

The young man was bearded and robed and explained that his wife was pregnant and they needed a room for the night.

He commented later, "We wanted to show what would happen when a poor young couple dressed like Joseph and Mary tried to get a room nearly 2,000 years after the birth of Christ—fully expecting a refusal as cold as the snow outside."

Instead, Holiday Inn's night manager handed them a key to room 101, inquired if the donkey would need any special attention, and offered them a free meal. "We weren't very hungry, so I asked him if we could have some drinks and you know what, he sent them around. It sure didn't happen this way 2,000 years ago."

How's that for one-upmanship?

12/15/71

Before Christmas I was tempted to write this editorial but resisted for fear it would be misinterpreted.

Despite all the plausible and applauded company programs against gift getting and giving by those who do business with one another, and despite the Internal Revenue's ceiling on the value of presents, I still like the custom.

One railroad, with a unique trademark, every year sends to people who are its friends and customers a clever, always varied present that incorporates this symbol. The whole Forbes family is happy that Pop is on the list.

The head of a brokerage firm sends to certain customers and friends a gift subscription to *Réalités*, a superb English-language magazine, edited, produced, and printed in France. The recipients love it.

Across my desk come some wonderful calendars, occasionally ashtrays, and other office-usable things.

I don't feel bribed. I don't feel bought.

I feel thought of. And I like it.

1/1/65

With the holidays past and such thanks as are due having been duly delivered, it's once again time to ruminate on the business practices of gift giving.

Nearly everybody seems to be against it—except the vendors, the recipients, and me.

A counter philosophy was well expressed in a leaflet from Brown & Gage, a Cleveland printing company—

> In line with other large corporations we wish to state our policy regarding Xmas gifts.
>
> We will accept all gifts regardless of size and price. As a matter of fact, the more expensive the gift, the better. Do not be afraid of sending something too lavish. It's better to have poor taste than to appear cheap.

(It's a joke, you literate readers.)

1/15/71

Food for Thought

The ifs, whens, whats, and how muches of tipping constitute one of the major minor decisions that almost daily face businessmen. Probably, more stuff and guff have been written on this subject than on many more important problems.

In *Forbes* magazine's Restaurant Guide, I wrote the following observations. Though the specifics deal with the

subject of restaurants, the general principles are applicable
in every other area that involves tipping.

The notion that tipping is optional and the amount dis-
cretionary is as quaint as the soul who might try it. Short
of being angered to the point of fisticuffs or other forms
of mayhem, if you last in a restaurant long enough to be
served and get the check, the basic rules are simple:

Fifteen percent of the bill for the waiter; another 5
percent of the bill for the captain in the places where he
hands you the menu, takes the order, makes the salad, and
generally works at the job; $1 per bottle for the wine
steward; and/or a buck for the bartender if he has made
several drinks.

The thought that you can walk out without tipping
if you have been dissatisfied is wonderful, but you'd best
leave it to Walter Mitty.

As for all that malarkey about being super careful
not to overtip—it's malarkey.

Did you ever hear any complaints from anyone you
did overtip?

The original John D. Rockefeller always tipped a
dime and got away with it. That was before anybody
knew how rich he was or who he was, and a dime was a
dime in those long-ago days.

After they knew who he was and how rich he was,
a dime from him was worth much more as a souvenir to
keep or to sell.

Now, however, unless you are the original John D.
Rockefeller, forget about tipping dimes.

If you really receive exceptional attention from the
captain or the waiter or the bartender, or a super smile
and wink from the hatcheck girl, the only way you can
express the warmth you feel is by tipping more than the
rule.

If you really dig the particular restaurant and plan

to use it often, the surest way to be sure of having your name remembered, of getting a good table or the first available table, of being made very welcome, is to occasionally tip the majordomo and the others a bit more than required.

For no strange reason this makes all concerned more than usually glad to see you coming.

After all, if you're going to be spending $20 or $30 for two at lunch and $30 or $40 for two at dinner, allowing two or three extra dollars in the tips shouldn't make or break you.

It can, though, double the enjoyment.

3/1/70

After a dozen days at sea last summer, I was shocked to discover that another eight pounds had been added to an excess in weight. It scared me into doing what multimillions of Americans do from time to time—diet.

I looked around for the easiest one available and came up with low carbohydrates. After several faithful weeks the eight pounds eventually went away. When reporting this to my perspicacious spouse, she remarked, "You think low carbohydrates did it. I have news for you. You simply have been eating less, and that's the *only* thing that did it."

When you consider the uncounted tens of millions of dollars that we spend annually to get fat and to lose it, 'tis appalling. Cookbooks and dieting books keep most publishers profitable; doctors wax on overweight counseling; drug companies pay dividends from the profits on products to deal with the results of excess weight as well as the weight itself; gymnasiums and gimcrack exercise gadgets proliferate; "health" spas spring up like scales; and older men who should know better make personal sport activities a fetish.

We could go on and on and on with the industries and the profitable activities that result from people concerned with excess pounds. Yet if all were to take my good wife's advice, think of the savings!

Eat less and walk more.

3/1/73

For generations Americans have been weaned to the words, "Now drink your milk." In my youth, as I recall, all that was needed to be an All-American football hero was the consumption of at least a quart of milk with every meal. Milk made the man. In fact, between doctors and the dairy industry, the cow was rapidly replacing the dog as man's best friend.

How Now Brown Cow!

The beasts may still be sacred in India, but the poly-saturated old things are no longer safe on Main Street, America.

Cholesterol's done it.

I don't quite understand what cholesterol is, but it sounds like a cross between a chigger and fallout. Whatever it is, it seems that cows spread it around disguised as milk, and all these generations we've been pumping poison into the kids. No wonder all our forebears are dead.

It's gotten so I don't even know how to talk to my children at the breakfast table. There were always only two proper things for a proper American father to say to his proper offspring at breakfast anyway: "Did you brush your teeth?" and "Drink your milk!" With our morning together-ness mealtime conversation now cut in half there are long periods of nervous silence, which I'm not sure are any good for one's health either.

Things weren't much improved the other day when the eight-year-old defended his negative to my "Did you brush your teeth?" by "There's chloroform in the water now and this fills in the cavities, so you don't need toothbrushes any more."

The ten-year-old said the eight-year-old meant chlorophyll. Somebody else said it was cholesterol, and my wife said that if cholesterol was now in both milk and water, we were going to have a very high liquor bill if we had to start pouring scotch for everyone at the breakfast table.

My oldest son, who reads, said it was fluorine in the water and that it prevented cavities instead of filling them, but that some cities voted down fluoridation because too much of it was also fatal.

I have found the only way a parent can win an argument with children is to lose his temper and be arbitrary, so I ordered the nontoothbrusher to go do it.

"Tell him, Pop, that if he doesn't, you'll kill him by making him drink his milk," suggested his gleeful sister.

Frankly, I don't know how the presidents of National Dairy, Borden, the Cattlemen's Association, the Dairymen's Association manage to sleep nights. In fact, maybe they don't. Maybe they're all up all night working to develop a polyunsaturated cow.

The whole thing may seem udderly ridiculous but, you know, it is a food fashion shift involving billions of dollars.

9/1/62

We Americans have been long famed for what is referred to as our Madison Avenue techniques—the ability to market successfully through advertising. One of the industry's classic case histories concerns an adman's inspiration to "sell the sizzle, not the steak." It has been such an undisputed success that it is now all but impossible to get a good steak anywhere in the country: lots of sizzle, lots of charcoal flavor (now available from spray-on cans), lots of parsley, and in the middle under some tired vegetables, a dried piece of beef.

8/1/61

We have long believed that man's most sensitive nerve is the pocketbook.

Things have changed, my friends.

Quite inadvertently, I put my finger on an even more tender spot. I don't know quite what to call it. The steak nerve?

A month ago here I made one of those sweeping, reader-irritating observations that "to have a really good steak anywhere between the East Coast and the West Coast is virtually impossible."

Nothing I have written in years has brought such an avalanche of charcoal-burned letters. I have been denounced on some of the best editorial pages of the great beef states of the west West and the Middle West. One columnist, Will Jones of the Minneapolis *Tribune*, wrote in reference to yours truly: "The man is to be pitied, for he's obviously never been to Minneapolis, where it's virtually impossible *not* to get a good steak. . . . To hell with him. . . . Let him enjoy his ignorance. Listen to how he babbles. . . ." Mr. Jones goes on to declare "that something has got to be done" about the fact that in every area but New York a particular slice of beef is referred to as "a New York cut."

Sociologists, I suppose, would draw one conclusion about this phenomenon of American steak sensitivity, psychologists still another, and economists yet another. For my part, however, I'm just happy to have received a lot of names of places to try steaks all over the country. The next time, driving west *avec ma famille*, we'll have a whole new set of objectives for each day's run.

6/15/66

Why do you suppose so many people seem to prefer big lobsters to small ones? In addition to costing much more, big ones invariably are much tougher. They had to be to get big in their world—which in terms of survival is not too unlike our own.

3/1/73

Antidote to/for whiners: wine.

3/1/73

What is so rare as a properly ripe avocado?

3/1/73

Recently, a San Francisco papermaker named Crown Zellerbach ran some large advertisements with this headline: IF YOU RAN A PAPER COMPANY, HOW WOULD YOU TREAT A GUY WHO SUGGESTED BREAD SHOULD BE WRAPPED IN PLASTIC?

I don't know how I would treat a guy who suggested bread should be wrapped in plastic, but I sure as heck would strike a medal for the guy who suggests that they should stop making the bread itself of plastic.

How long has it been since you've had a piece of bread that tasted like bread?

4/15/67

Many maître d's get so full of themselves they forget to see that their hungry customers are served. Under such circumstances the customers usually have had more than enough before they get fed—fed up, one might say, if one were tempted to pun.

10/15/68

Have you ever noticed that in a busy, crowded store or during the busiest, most crowded hours in a restaurant the service is usually faster and more efficient? At the least busy times, when the fewest customers are present, the service is slowest, poorest.

As to why, I haven't the faintest.

But some psychologist or efficiency expert, I'm sure, could provide us with some esoteric explanation.

Anyway, it's a pain in the neck in a half-empty store or an almost empty restaurant not to be able to catch one of the many empty eyes all over the place.

10/1/66

We all deplore surly waiters and haughty captains, who can do as much to bring on ulcers as some of the food they serve. But, as you may have noticed, some customers sometimes can be so rude, crude, and arrogantly unattractive that even saintly thee and me would be tempted to spill every course in their laps.

You know some of the types—psychologists tell us it represents insecurity or something—who sniff and complain about every dish and think sending things back impresses witnesses. As indeed it does—unfavorably.

Others who snap their fingers imperiously to summon waiters and who address them in a tone of voice usually reserved for mothers-in-law.

Oh, we the public can be exasperating, inconsiderate, and sometimes bearing a bearing beyond bearing. It's not unreasonable to suppose that, after several such in a day and many in a week, sometimes all hands in a restaurant get fed up, so to speak.

Maybe if we mind our own manners a bit more, more waiters will find it easier to mind theirs.

12/1/71

Only Natural— People and Human Nature

Everyone loves a "character"—so long as one's exposure to whatever it is that makes a character a character isn't too often or too long.

Behavior that would be branded as bad taste or bad manners or simply bad by us ordinary mortals becomes a charming idiosyncrasy or eccentricity if one is a genius or has jillions of dollars.

For instance, Steven Birmingham, in his fascinating book, *Our Crowd*, tells this anecdote about Adolph Lewisohn:

> As a host, Adolph insisted on a few prerogatives. Though he was more a listener than a talker, he did, whenever he had anything to say, demand that everyone else in the room be silent. He enjoyed playing bridge, but had a highly individual approach to the game. The following is a typical Lewisohn bridge contract:
>
> Lewisohn (dealer): "One club."
> West: "Two diamonds."
> North: "Two spades."
> East: "Five diamonds."
> Lewisohn: "One club."
>
> The hand was played at one club.

Now, you must admit, that is delightful.
So long as it happened to three other people.

10/1/68

Don't we tend to think a quiet one is a wise one?

Whether it is a businessman or otherwise, at a corporate round table or a nineteenth hole rap, the ones who talk the most and who sometimes say something tend to pitch their prose to the quiet ones. The premise is that the silent one is a thinker, or at least a listener (rare breed!).

I am coming to think, though, that more often than not the silent one is so because he has nothing to say. He really doesn't even have to listen so long as he looks as though he is.

I am sure you remember in school days the nonparticipant in classroom instruction wasn't rewarded high marks on the premise that he knew more. He scored low on the premise that he had not done his homework. Very probably, more often that same standard should be applied in executive sessions.

Silence may be golden in exhaust pipes, but not necessarily in high-priced executives.

8/15/72

Most times I am glad that people are more apt to be tolerant of mistakes, more apt to be forgiving of failure than they are of perpetual rightness and great success.

What is it about the person who is always right, the person who constantly succeeds, that so irritates the rest of us mortals?

7/15/70

Most of us maintain we are not superstitious. Yet somehow we don't go out of our way to walk under ladders, but not to. We joke a bit about Friday the thirteenth, and when no one's looking, keep our fingers crossed.

When we take to the highways, the airways, or the sea for long journeys, we stoutly reassure all and any who seem to care: "Don't worry. When my time has come, it's come and there's nothing to be done about it." Only we mutter a silent prayer that contradicts this verbal bravado.

Have you noticed in office buildings and hotels and even table seating lists that thirteen is always fourteen?

Superstitious?

That's for the ignorant, the tribal, the backward people.

And the rest of us.

11/1/67

I haven't a clue about the biology or the psychology involved when a person dissolves into tears, but it is quite fascinating to note what turns 'em on.

There are wives who can cascade over a late husband and a burned dinner, and equally pour tears of joy over a new bonnet or a renovated bathroom.

Then there's the Solitary Tear school, with a self-control that leaves me enrapt with admiration . . . you know, the lone "hurt" tear that wells and slowly descends.

In India and some other places the noise of wailing rather than wetness does the trick. Half the funeral expense goes to hire loud weepers.

We also have the heaving Sobbers at Sad Movies who, on getting home, heartlessly rap their kids over the head with a frying pan because they used up the peanut butter making sandwiches while Mom was at the triple flick.

Too, it seems to me, more people cry at weddings than at funerals. Maybe it is because they regard the former as a premature version of the latter, and the latter as a form of . . . emancipation? (Darling, I am not talking about us, of course.)

Water on the knee is something doctors know all about. Water in and out of the eye is entirely something else again.

I was put in mind of this whole matter by a quotation in one of the interviews in that absorbing book *Division Street*, where a woman with not much besides problems in her life says, "I don't cry for sorrow. That I can swallow and hold. But for real joy, I can cry."

9/1/67

It never ceases to amaze me how so many other people like so many of the same things you and I like—praise, love, holidays, good pay, vacations, and so forth.

Quite a coincidence.

5/15/69

Have you ever noticed how many people long and harmoniously married get to look quite a lot alike? The next time you see a picture of a couple celebrating their fiftieth wedding anniversary, look at it closely and you'll see.

8/15/72

If you dislike a man and want him to dislike you, here's a surefire way to get the job done—

On being introduced in a small gathering or large, in the course of the minutes of unavoidable conversation, be sure to avoid looking at him. While he attempts conversation with you, or you mumble at him, look over his shoulder and around the room at others. When not looking past him, keep glancing at your wristwatch.

A very brief while of this and—presto!—your mission is accomplished.

7/1/70

In case you missed it, here's a fabulous Associated Press interview in the course of which Mrs. Jolene Gearin's every comment should spark your own commentary.

San Pedro, Calif. (AP)—Jolene Gearin says she was poor before she inherited $200,000 four years ago. Now she's poor again and cheerfully admits, "We blew it."

Mrs. Gearin was living in a $75-a-month apartment when she learned she would inherit $200,000 from the estate of her father, Chester Hanson. With her husband, Leonard, a merchant marine seaman, and their four children, she waited through two years of court action for the money. Then taxes took part of it.

"But when it came, it really wore us out spending it," she recalls. "We were just exhausted. We couldn't spend it fast enough."

Where did the money go?

"We bought cars and motorcycles for the boys, and a truck, and a $2,000 hi-fi . . . and clothes, and we put a down payment on a house, and the girls and I had all our teeth capped, and I had my breasts lifted . . .

"And, oh yes, we bought ski equipment . . . and we traveled . . . we put 200,000 miles on one of the cars in one year . . . and we all saw a psychiatrist . . . I invested $10,000 in the stock market and lost $4,000 . . . and we spent $5,000 on new furniture, a washer and a dryer, small appliances . . .

"We paid cash for everything. . . ."

Lessons learned? "You can sure waste a lot of money on cars, and the stock market is a bad investment," Mrs. Gearin said.

Lasting effects? "When we found out about the money, it brought the family together. It was the first time in our lives that we really worked and planned together . . .

"After the money was gone we started fighting. They kept saying, 'Why didn't we spend it this way?' But they were all there to spend it and we all had fun . . .

"It made us all different. The family needed this. . . . But all of a sudden when we realized we were broke, we decided there was a brand new world out there. . . . We all got smart. We realize now that the fun is over."

1/15/72

In the lingo of our land, one who really knows how to do superbly what he's doing is known as a pro. It's always a treat to see a pro in action, whether he's a bootblack who knows how, a top management man who is truly a master at his job, a golfer who invariably puts the ball where he intended to, or a hunter who does the same with his shot, or, rarest of all, a waiter who doesn't stand around waiting.

Knowing, caring, enjoying, pride—all are ingredients of the pro. If you know any, never begrudge paying well to see them or be served by them. They are a rare, inspiring breed.

3/1/68

One way to find out what you need to know and don't know is to ask those who do.

It's remarkable, though, how many of us through misplaced pride or stubbornness or shyness or plain stupidity hesitate or refuse to pop questions that need answering.

How often while driving to an unfamiliar destination have you and your wife argued whether the turn should be to the right or the left—or should you go on to the next light? As time passes and temperatures rise it becomes harder and harder to ask someone who might know.

How often have you noticed people pounding around in an unfamiliar place looking for the rest room? They'd rather walk a mile and try every door than ask.

In business failing to ask is often more fatal. The man who won't ask what he doesn't know either has to fake the answer or duck the question. In either case he limits his future. After all, who wants a man in a position of responsibility who is too dumb to seek answers from those who know more about some matters than he does?

Of course, asking a question reveals that you don't know the answer.

Failure to ask questions about what you want or need to know, however, reveals much more—all bad.

5/1/68

Occasionally, we all inherit, or are given, or get something or several things that are too good to use for a variety of

seemingly sound but really quite silly reasons—they're heir-
looms or they're too rare or too expensive or too fragile or too
pretty or too this and/or too that.

The result is heirloom linen handed down from generation to generation that falls apart when some benighted
heiress decides eventually to air it. Or the treasured dish or
glass or other breakable thing that finally falls shatteringly
between grabbing claimants.

While I must admit to being glad that our past generations saved some things that we now enjoy, we *are* enjoying them by using them instead of just carefully storing them
for our kids in turn to store away for theirs.

Museums are for that.

Untouchable, unused beautiful things are a waste.

4/1/71

Happiness is sometimes something in the mailbox.

Preferably, of course, a check. Or a real honest-to-good-
ness letter from family, friend, or even foe. Just so long as
it's by hand rather than written by computer or printing
press. Then there are bills, magazines, and bank statements.

Finally and mostly, there's what so many of us unthink-
ingly call junk mail—offering magazines and books and
records and food and club memberships and credit cards and
insurance and just about everything that one needs or
(mostly) doesn't.

The fashion of complaining about the quantity of this
unsolicited mail is about to have results: There will be far
less of it for most people. Because, seemingly, public opinion
supports fantastic increases in the postage costs for third-
class mail.

To make such mailings pay off now, mailers must prune
and prune mailing lists, so that if you haven't bought much

of anything by mail in recent months, your name is out, your mailbox emptier.

Sure, that's what everyone says he wants.

But do you really mean it?

Lonesomeness can be an empty mailbox. When you're off most of the lists and no more costly free offers and rending appeals are there for you to open—believe me, you'll feel a bit more out of this world.

3/1/72

Without Goren, communications at the bridge table would probably still be in the caveman, that is, Culbertson, age. As a bridger who substitutes avidity for capability, I have evolved the Forbes' Bridge Rule:

Never apologize for a boo-boo—too soon.

Time after time after time after doing something of patent stupidity in either the bidding or the playing, I have immediately showered the table with apologies and self-condemnation. Only to have the apologized act turn out to have had no bad effect and, occasionally, a good one.

Thus learning to bite one's tongue, learning not to say "sorry" too soon, can often result in having a boner pass for a bit of genius.

Come to think of it, this Forbes' Bridge Rule is not without application to the conduct of business:

Never apologize for a boo-boo—too soon.

3/1/70

Youth and Age

For the young the future lies ahead.
    For the Now age the future is here.
    For the old the future is remembrance of things past.

1/1/73

This summer my wife and I and brood broke some wondrous fresh bread at lunch in a lovely Maine harbor with Clarence Dillon, the legendary Wall Street wizard of many decades. He is now eighty-six, and we hadn't seen him for a long time. His eyes had lost none of their sparkle; his perceptions were as acute as ever; and his lively interest in an infinite variety of things was as keen as always.

With cane, cap, and ruddy complexion, he belied his age by the enthusiastic warmth of his greeting.

"Mr. Dillon, you look wonderful!" said I, and meant it.

"Malcolm, there are three ages of man.

"Youth.

"Middle age.

"And . . . 'My, how well you look!' "

11/15/68

Youth is wasted on youth, according to an old saying. But I think it's quite the other way 'round—the advantages of age are wasted on old people.

To be granted the wisdom that usually accrues from several decades of living while one is actually young in body and spirit—ah!—there's the combination!

5/1/71

The wife of one of New York's most eminent lawyers and her sister were discussing what to give their aging, ailing father for Christmas a couple of years ago. "I'm going to give Daddy time—much more time," she said. Her sister later commented to me: "On a moment's reflection, I realized what a wonderful and rare gift that would be."

It's completely true, you know.

We love our old folks, but have or think we have little time to give them.

When one is quite old and has only time, a little bit more of it from friends and loved ones is the most precious gift he can receive and that we can give.

12/15/72

Three kids—I'd guess about eight years old—were shining shoes on home-made equipment the other day on one of New York's poshest avenues. Their faces shone like the shoes they finished.

Needing a shine, I stopped. As I sat down a portly, profitable-looking tycoon type was just getting up.

He proffered the boy a $5 bill, and naturally the youngster didn't have change for that much.

"Okay, son, I'll get it changed and bring you back the quarter."

When I was ready to leave almost ten minutes later, the creep hadn't yet returned. There were a dozen shops within a minute's distance where change could have been had. Instead, the shoeshine boy was.

8/1/69

Are you prepared to drop dead?

If so, if you've done estate planning and written a will, you are the exception rather than the rule.

Why do so many smart *hombres* fail to get ready for demise?

Maybe it's because so many people think that to write a will is to invite the event one is thus prepared for. Like my wife's reaction when I mentioned during the course of a 2,400-mile drive from Wyoming to New York that we had gone most of the way without a flat. "Now you've done it! You've tempted fate! Now we'll have a flat for sure," she wailed. (We did.)

Whatever it is, most of the very people you would think would be the first to write a will and/or do estate planning don't do it at all.

With no thought, no plan, no will, they leave their widow, their children, their heirs in a mess, the straightening out of which often dissipates monies sorely needed by loved ones left behind.

First National City Bank's trust department officers sometimes test to get an idea of people's knowledge of estates and taxes. It is in the form of four statements, each to be marked true or false. Try it yourself and see how little *you* know on the subject!

	TRUE	FALSE
LIFE INSURANCE is not subject to tax		
JOINT PROPERTY one-half value is taxable		

SAVINGS ACCOUNTS
    no tax if "in trust" for
    children		

STOCK OPTIONS
    no tax if not exercised
    before death		

Not more than 10 percent of those surveyed got all four correct, and 25 percent had all four wrong.

The correct answer is false in all four cases.

If you haven't, get busy now with your banker and your lawyer. Proper planning will save your heirs not only money, but headaches and heartache.

The only ones jinxed if you don't are those you care most about.

9/15/64

People who live a hundred years or more are often inter-viewed, and more often than not cackle gleefully that their longevity is the result of misspent youth, excessive sex, smok-ing, and drinking.

Which makes most of us feel a bit better.

Now some just-completed study of old-timers says it isn't so, that those who live more than a century almost all led sensible early-to-bed lives, just as doctors and parents have always said that we should.

Disillusioning, isn't it?

3/1/71

This subject of oldsters came up at a luncheon here with that dynamic Canadian banker W. Earl McLaughlin. Observed the head of the $11 billion Royal Bank, "Life expectancy of 100-year-olds is quite good. Very seldom do you hear of any-one that age dying."

3/1/71

One of the venerable greats of American journalism is E. K. Gaylord, the spry and sparkling 100-year-old proprietor of the *Daily Oklahoman* and the Oklahoma City *Times*. His mind is as quick and sharp as any I know, and he moves with a sprightliness that most people half his age don't manage.

I asked him what I suppose for the past decade or two countless others have asked him: "How do you stay so healthy? What's your secret? What's your formula?"

He chuckled and with eyes twinkling replied: "My doctor once asked me that and said he wanted to share with his patients my prescription for a long life and good health. I said I'd tell him, but I bet any sum he wanted that he wouldn't pass on to any of his patients my answer.

"I told him, 'For more years than I can remember, I have been going to a chiropractor once a week.' "

Now before you doctor readers rage at me, that's a quotation—which isn't the same thing as a recommendation.

4/15/73

Some of the greening Green Young have positively Positive Thoughts. Through their glum gloom about the glue of Life as lived by the rest of us comes this gleam in the form of a best-seller shirt patch:

"Today is the first day of the rest of your life."

6/1/71

At a neighbor's dinner party the other evening, one contemporary was lamenting the prospect of an operation.

Another was audibly nursing his golf-strained back.

Commented a third guest: "After fifty it's just patch, patch, patch."

6/1/71

One of the most tragic things in American society today is the way employers tend increasingly to turn up their noses at aging job seekers. It is a social problem full of heartaches and pathos. It is an economic problem as well: With a booming economy pushing employment to the limits, every able-bodied man lost to the work force means that much more pressure of inflation.

Just how ridiculous the situation has become is illustrated by some figures released by the Department of Labor. They show that the actual turning point—the birthday at which the American begins to find his age a real handicap in job getting—is neither sixty-five nor fifty-five nor even fifty. It is forty-five! Employers, in other words, seem to think that the useful life span is not the Biblical three score and ten but two score and five. Too old at forty-five? No biologist, psychologist, or sociologist would agree that most people are worn out at forty-five, but that is what the employment statistics seem to say.

Why is this so? How old, really, is *too* old? There is simply no pat answer to this question, but the reasons given by employers for rejecting older job applicants throw little light on this subject. Sometimes employers turn down older workers on the basis of physical requirements necessary for a longshoreman or a paratrooper but not for a file clerk. Sometimes the employer is afraid to offer a man a lesser job than he formerly held—even though the individual concerned has no such scruple. Occasionally, too, the older man's own defeatism and discouragement hurt him in a society where success is too often accepted simply at face value.

But these are really only prejudices and misconceptions. A little understanding can clear them up. But sometimes another argument is raised against the hiring of "older" workers—and sometimes raised in firms otherwise noteworthy for their enlightened employee relations. This is the question of how much it would add to the pension fund or other "fringe" benefit burden to hire a middle-aged man. The argument for this point of view is simple—although somewhat questionable. Since the older man is closer to retirement age than the younger man, it will presumably take a larger annual contribution to fund his pension. Also, the argument runs, he can be expected to give fewer years' service for the training investment the company makes in him. Thus many companies which otherwise realize the value of the older worker in terms of stability, loyalty, and devotion, write him off as an uneconomic proposition.

Is the employer taking on an older worker really letting

himself in for heavy pension and other costs? The evidence is not entirely clear, but an older worker could well be something of a financial burden under the terms of many pension plans.

All this has a corollary which affects the middle-aged worker in quite a different way: Once he has built up a decade or so of equity in a pension plan, he is understandably reluctant to change jobs, if changing involves the loss of his accumulated pension rights. This may cause him to turn down a better job. Thus we are not only deprived of the services of useful older people, but we are dooming others to work at less than their full capacity.

Insofar as this is true, I think there is something wrong with pension plans. *Forbes* is all for the basic idea of pensions with all it implies for security, stability, and peace of mind.

But stability is one thing, stagnation is another. What we seek is security under free enterprise, not an extension of the welfare state mentality. Vesting of pension rights may or may not be the answer. But some way must be found so that pension funds will neither encourage employers to regard the middle-aged as too old nor freeze the ambitious younger man in a position below his potential capacity.

7/15/57

When it comes to youth, marketing men these days are suffering from the damnedest myopia, self-manufactured mystique that I've ever seen. 'Cause there are so many of them, everybody making and selling things these days aims his pitch and project at the young. (No, that doesn't include you, dear thirty-year-oldster and older.)

But unless you're making soda pop, souped-up cars, screech sounds, old military uniforms, underground newspapers, pot festivals, or pot without the festivals, you're wasting a bundle pitching your wares at the young.

So far as they're concerned, you and what you make or sell just ain't where it's at, and your attempts to cash in on our young, cashless society are as absurd from a business point of view as they are to the objects of your blandishments. One of these days somebody on Madison Avenue is going to wake up to the fact that the young don't want—presently—what we've got, and haven't got the dough to buy it.

So, why not aim at where the market is? The old men of twenty-five and thirty, the middle-aged forties, the cats of fifty and sixty, who've got the wheel at office and home (I'm speaking metaphorically, dear wives); even those in their seventies and the toddlers in their eighties have dough and are spending it on the premise that they may not live forever. The kid, pardon me, youth market, will grow up to be like the rest of us eventually—caught in the glue of all the things that make life comfortable.

Meantime, as a market, forget it.

3/15/70

The other evening around 10 P.M. we were finishing dinner in a fine, famed San Francisco restaurant, when a relatively young parental pair came in with their three youngsters—two girls about nine and seven and a boy of about five or six. The little boy had on long pants and a bow tie, and the girls were dressed the way you'd think middle teeners might be —in high heels and so forth.

It always seems to me such a waste, such a missing of the point when parents try to make big kids out of little ones. Dressing a five-year-old to look like a twenty-five-year-old isn't really cute, except maybe for a costume party.

Long dresses and long pants and high heels and all the

rest of it come soon enough. There's a time—all too brief as it too soon becomes apparent to parents—to be little, a time to be in between, a time to be a teener, a time to be grown up, and a time to be old.

Let each have its season. Rushing anything, including the stages of life, is almost always a mistake.

Let the little be little.

Old comes soon enough.

10/1/69

Young people who are not intolerant of all things wrong in the world are old before their time.

When else except when young does one see so clearly the bad and unjust that is everywhere? When else does one feel so strongly that so much can and should be done to put it all right?

Intolerance of the intolerable is always applaudable.

But it is irritating when young people show a screaming, stomping intolerance of those who don't agree with the In Thinking Of The Season. (They seem unaware of the fact that the In Thinking Of The Season changes almost seasonally.)

The windmill tilters demand that far-out voices be heard on campuses and in the parks. They parade and protest-placard all the places that govern city, country, and world. Great.

But the worm in the can is the vehemence with which they deny either integrity or audience to the disagreers-with-them. Guitar pluckers and campus criers for justice are always in vogue when In Protest. The minority in the country and on the downtown campuses are those few who express support for prevailing policies and politicians.

Instead of proving they can practice what they question,

the young egg their contemporaries who disagree. They up-turn the cars of square speakers who show up on their scene. They shout down and de-shirt the minority.

It is all quite discouraging.

But I suppose instead of taking hemlock, we ought to take heart that today's youth is not one bit different from its several generations of predecessors.

Which, I guess, includes us.

7/1/67

To young people everything looks permanent, established —and in their eyes practically everything should be, needs to be changed.

To older people almost everything seems to change, and in their view almost nothing should.

Anyone in doubt about the generation gap?

4/1/69

Funeral directors may soon join barbers in bewailing the prevailing mores of today's younger generation.

On the sensible premise that funerals are for the living and are unlikely to be a matter of great moment to the dead, the Now generation opts for quick, clean simplicity in dis-posing of our generation when we are dead—officially cer-tified as such, that is.

Increasingly, cremation's the thing. Those who qualify can be described as having gone Up in smoke.

The passing of the wake and other expensive, elaborate mourning celebrations will be missed by neither the Gone nor those left (freed?) to go on. In this instance at least, can we agree that the new generation makes more sense than our own?

2/1/71

In the course of conversations with astute Sundstrand Chairman Bruce Olson, he mentioned one of his bad decisions.

In 1962 Sundstrand decided to go into the manufacture of styrene foam coffins because it already made the machinery with which they were produced. "The whole idea made rational sense," says Olson, "but was a complete flop because we didn't realize that people *want* to pay a lot of money for coffins."

Make your own moral out of that one.

4/15/69

One group of doctors who still make house calls: coroners.

7/1/72

Memorabilia

The combination of moving offices and a fiftieth anniversary leads to much rummaging in dusty files. In the course of cleaning out the closets, we've turned up many fascinating footnotes on the events and people that made American business history.

For instance—

My father had heard tell that Thomas A. Edison first became interested in inventing "incandescent light" as a result of anger at the gas man who had finally turned off the gas in Edison's laboratory because the bill was too long unpaid.

My father queried Mr. Edison, "Is this true?"

The reply in pencil by Mr. Edison was written on the letter of inquiry, dated September 7, 1920 (*see next page*).

So much history of necessity is hearsay; so much about those who made history inevitably grows in the telling, often is more apocryphal than factual.

This note, in the hand of the man who lit the world, is the fascinating sort of thing which makes monumental happenings seem real, human, understandable: "In substance it's true, I was paying a sheriff $5 a day to postpone a judgement, on my small factory. Then came the gas man and he cut off my gas. That made me so mad that I read up gas Technique & Economics and decided I would try if electricity couldn't be made to replace gas and give them a run for their money and I stuck to it for 4 years but I was so poor an economist that I didn't hurt them at all except lately—40 years—Edison."

6/15/67

The following two letters were written to my father by George Eastman, founding father of Eastman Kodak. At the time the second letter was written, I was two months old.

Particularly intriguing, I think, is the last line. The man whose inventive genius made a mammoth business out of people making pictures of each other liked "to keep out of the limelight."

Fascinating.

EDISON

With all thy getting, get Understanding

FORBES

Published Every Two Weeks

299 BROADWAY
NEW YORK

Sept. 7, 1920.

Mr. William H. Meadowcroft,
Thomas A. Edison, Inc.,
Orange, N. J.

Dear Mr. Meadowcroft:

Is this true?

Or isn't it?

It is interesting--if true.

Yours very sincerely,

B C Forbes

BCF/GW

Forbes

In substance its true, I was paying a Sheriff $5. a day to postpone a judgement, on my small factory then Came the gas man & he cut off my gas, That made me so mad that I read up gas Technology & Economics & decided I would try if Electricity couldnt be made to replace gas & give them a run for their money

& I stuck to it for 4 yrs but I was so poor an Economist that I didnt twist them at all except lately — 40 yrs — Edison

70

EASTMAN KODAK COMPANY

ROCHESTER, N.Y.

December 27th, 1916

Mr. B. C. Forbes

New York City

Dear Sir:—

In looking up the dates that I gave you I find they are as follows:

I began the manufacture of dry plates in September, 1880.

Formed a partnership with Mr. Henry A. Strong January 1, 1881.

The Eastman Dry Plate & Film Co. was incorporated October 1, 1884. Capital $200,000. Increased to $300,000 May 25, 1885. This additional capital was used to buy the European patents from Strong, Eastman and Walker.

The first roll holders with paper film were put out in April, 1885. Stripping film October, 1887.

The first Kodak in June, 1888.

Transparent films in August, 1889.

Daylight films in December, 1894.

Motion picture film, 1895.

The developing machine August, 1902.

Non-curling film, 1904.

Autographic Kodaks June, 1914.

Under another cover I am sending you a picture of the Martin building, in the upper stories of which the business of the Kodak Company had its origin; a general view of the Kodak Park Works, taken from a kite early in 1909 (the floor space of this plant has been doubled since this picture was taken); and a picture of the general offices. Perhaps this latter picture would be better to contrast with that of the Martin building than the kite picture.

Yours very truly,

Geo Eastman

EASTMAN KODAK COMPANY
ROCHESTER, N.Y.

October 14th, 1919

Mr. B. C. Forbes
   New York City

Dear Mr. Forbes:

In accordance with your request I am sending you a recent photograph.

In considering a man for employment the question whether he is thrifty is almost always an important one, no matter what the job is. If he cannot take care of his own affairs it is presumptive evidence that he will be weak in the conduct of others'. It takes a mighty good excuse to explain why a man is in debt. I was brought up to fear debt and as a matter of fact in the early years I always saved something every year no matter what my salary was. Having formed the habit I have managed to conduct my business so that we have never had to borrow any money but that is not always practicable or perhaps wise. If a man is really thrifty and needs to borrow money his reputation for thrift is his greatest asset next to honesty.

I never made any talk on thrift, or for that matter on anything else, and as you know, like to keep out of the limelight.

Yours very truly,
Geo Eastman

3/1/66

From the *Forbes* files, marked "Confidential"—1923:

Feb. 28, 1923

Dear Mr. Forbes:

I was very much pained to see your article in the press this morning in which you say, in discussing the Rural Credits Legislation, "Mr. Hoover blasted, by his famous dissertation on

Europe's ability to pay her war debts, whatever reputation he may previously have been accorded as a financier."

I, of course, do not lay claim to be a financier but I do lay claim to the fact that I have never formulated a proposition of importance without consultation with the best independent experts that are available.

In the matter of the rural credit legislation you will see by the enclosed letter which I recently wrote to Congressman Anderson that this legislation was formulated by financial experts. It was approved by the very people who now disapprove of it. The reasons why they have abandoned it are another story.

In the matter of the Allied Debt, I cannot believe you have ever read the statement which I made on this subject, copy of which I also send you. In formulating this proposition I also took the advice of the best independent authorities in the country and I recognize that I subjected myself to the malice of the organized propaganda for cancellation. Nevertheless, the success of the British negotiations are to a very material degree due to the firm attitude here taken. Beyond all this I could demonstrate to your satisfaction, in ten minutes, that the capital sum of the continental debt can be paid and I can well support the hypothesis set up in this statement that any concession as to abatement of interest should be a quid pro quo for such measures as will promote stability.

Having long admired your entire independent influence and clarity of thought in these matters I am indeed sorry that you have taken this attitude and I do believe that if you will take time to go into both questions you will find that there is a great deal more to be said on the other side than this quotation would indicate. I should be glad to see you some time.

Yours faithfully,

Herbert Hoover
(Secretary of Commerce
Washington, D.C.)

Mar. 8, 1923

Dear Mr. Hoover:

About the last golf game I had at Pinehurst before returning to New York was with Frank Presbrey, who spoke a great deal about you, as a result of which I wrote the little squib enclosed.

On returning, I found your letter of the 28th of February.

Frankly, I was terribly disappointed when I read your speech on the repayment of European debts. Yes, I read it in full at the time. I could not see eye to eye with several of your arguments, and when I came to the statement, "I am convinced that the capital sum of these debts can be paid some time with the exception of say 5 per cent," I could hardly believe that such a statement could have been made by you.

Until I read this address of yours, I had found myself in agreement, so far as I can recall, with practically everything you had ever urged or recommended, and I had taken frequent occasion to express to others my very great admiration for, among many other things, your extraordinary sound judgment.

I don't believe you can quite understand how badly—I might say sad—I felt when this address was published. I take a very keen interest in men who are doing big things, and particularly in those whom I have got to know personally. Somehow, I feel very close to them.

I did so about you. Hence, the depth of my disappointment when you came out with something which struck me as being fundamentally unsound.

However, in the hurley-burley of daily life, one must be prepared for differences of opinions, disappointments, etc., and try to let them weigh upon one as lightly as possible.

I cordially share your hope that we may be able to have another talk in the very near future, and with kindest regards,

Yours very sincerely,

B. C. Forbes

Mar. 12, 1923

My dear Forbes:

Many thanks for your frank letter of March 8th. The time will come when you will, I am sure, come to recognize that not only was I right in the statement at Toledo, but that it was an effectual piece of public service.

I would like to take an hour to discuss it with you because I believe you will agree with me when I can show you some of the sub currents that flow in this matter.

Yours faithfully,
Herbert Hoover

7/15/66

Purely Personal

Forbes magazine was a sturdy two-year-old when its present president began the wailing he's kept up for the past forty-eight years. My own memory does not cover in much detail the first halcyon dozen years of *Forbes*' history. I vividly remember, though, that we were doing very well, because Christmas in 1928 included a long Packard for Mom to haul her five sons around in, and a Red Bug—a two-bucket-seated, battery-powered children's car—for us to fight over.

Things soon changed.

And how.

Several weeks of summer vacation during the Thirties I spent working at $15 a week in the *Forbes* office. A portion of this sum went to fare for a train that has long since ceased to run, and no socialist cheered louder than I when half-day Saturday work was eliminated.

In those rugged Depression summers, I worked in the "mail cage," where the envelopes were slit and the subscription payments extracted. Dad used to come pounding down the office aisle, pulling on his inevitable cigar, and pause long enough to ask, "How much today?" His expression never changed, though inevitably the answer was inadequate.

Except once.

That day the controller told him excitedly, "Mr. Forbes, you'll be happy to know that the ledger shows a slight profit this month!"

With the Scottish burr he never lost, my father turned to him and said, "Young man, I don't give a damn what your books show. Do we have any *money in the bank*?"

It was my first lesson in the meaning of cash flow.

In the deeper months of the Depression, no salaries were paid anyone at *Forbes* one week out of the month. That hurt. The employees of *Forbes* dubbed those seven payless days each month "Scotch week."

For most of three years, Dad wasn't able to cash a *Forbes* paycheck. He drew them, paid the tax, and stuck them away. He took enormous joy some years later in cashing every one.

Immediately upon discharge from the army, I eagerly

went to work for *Forbes*. A hundred dollars a week was awfully good compared with both army pay and the $15-a-week Depression pay (and since then I have taken advantage of being in a position to improve that particular wage).

Afflicted with the usual disease of youth, I soon was full of suggestions about how everything and anything could be done differently and "better." There was a limit to Dad's patience, though, when one day my suggestions included some ideas on how he could "improve" one of his editorials. I never knew that he knew the words he used to squelch that temerity.

He had, however, a wonderful approach about letting my late brother Bruce and me undertake costly changes or new ventures:

"I have enough put away to provide me with three square meals a day for the rest of my life. If you boys feel strongly enough that you are on sound ground, go ahead. But always keep in mind, it's *your* future that's at stake."

In 1947, I dreamt up and persuaded *Forbes* to publish a unique magazine, *Nation's Heritage*. Hardbound, it was huge and magnificent.

And unprofitable.

It was to be bimonthly and to sell for $125 a year.

It didn't.

After the third issue it was apparent we weren't going to be successful, and I recommended that we cease publication. Said my father: "You contracted to deliver six issues to subscribers. We will deliver six issues."

We did, at a great loss.

My father loved poker, and about once a month for many, many years he would gather some like-minded cronies at the Metropolitan Club in New York for a session. The "regulars" included the unmatched, wonderful W. Alton

Jones of Cities Service; Scripps Howard's Roy Howard; Metropolitan Life's Leroy Lincoln; Commonwealth & Southern's Wendell Willkie; Underwood's Phil Wagoner; and that total gentleman, Robert W. Woodruff of Coca-Cola. (One such evening got off to a sticky start when Bob Woodruff noticed that the bar tray had *Pepsi*-Colas on it.)

Occasionally Bruce or I was invited to join in when another pair of hands was needed. Dad's arrangements with us were simple: "I'll pay half your losses and you keep your winnings." This ensured maximum effort, maximum betting care on our part. The limit was $1, and I don't ever recall when an evening's loss exceeded $50. My father used to shake with delight in describing the moroseness with which Leroy Lincoln paid his invariable losses: "I never knew even a Scotsman who could unsnap his purse more reluctantly."

Memories don't really mean much except to those who hold them. For imposing a few of them upon you on this particular occasion, I apologize.

9/15/67

The sweeping tides of Normandy were the greatest and only allies the Nazis had in their fierce, desperate effort to repel Allied forces on D Day, June 6, 1944. The two of them combined to pile high the dead on Omaha Beach. Weeks later, when the front had been pushed back so that much of France was free, the outfit in which I was a machine gun section sergeant landed on and traipsed across the incredibly crowded stretch of sand. After bivouacking in the Normandy hedgerow country, we trucked by Red Ball Express across France and into battle near Amiens.

A little while ago I visited Omaha Beach for the second time in my life. In the intervening twenty-six years nearly

20,000 tides have come and gone, and little remains visible of the greatest military landing in man's history of endless warring. What's to be seen is mostly in a superb museum and a panoramic cemetery. The cemetery memorializes with dignity and grandeur the event and the dead, and moves one deeply.

Before they die less precipitously and/or in lesser purpose, Americans who can should visit World War II's Normandy Beach. Such seeing and remembering helps a man's perspective.

11/15/70

Daytimes, sometimes, I'm home. Like on weekends and holidays and a once-in-a-while hooky day. All the day long, whether it's upstairs in our chamber or downstairs in our kitchen, TV is on.

Half the time there's no one even in the room, and for a long time my first action was to shut the noisy thing off. Invariably, from out of sight, and *almost* out of sound, would come a wifey voice: "Hey, turn that back on!"

To my querulous query of "Why?" came the firm, illogical rejoinder, "Because I like it on."

The rationale was never quite clear to me until *The New York Times*' Dan Sullivan began a critique of daytime television with this illuminating paragraph: "Television critics who rap daytime programs for being even more stupid than the ones we get at night are, my wife tells me, missing the point. The function of daytime TV, she says, is neither to entertain nor instruct. It is to provide a pleasant background babble—rather like an indoor waterfall—as the American housewife goes about her chores. You're not supposed to watch it, for heaven's sake."

8/1/68

For the Praise-That-Won't-Go-To-Your-Head Department:

From our absent seventeen-year-old son, a note expressing appreciation for some needed wherewithal:

"You're the best mother and father I've ever had."

7/15/66

OUT OF THE MOUTHS OF BABES—NO WISDOM

One of the family ran across a fading Newark *Star-Ledger* that contained an interview of fifteen years ago with my wife while I was the Republican candidate for governor of New Jersey (and nosed out by a landslide). The feature was full of stuff a mother has to do daily in raising five youngsters, the oldest then nine and the youngest one and a half. It concluded with this paragraph: "None of the Forbes children was quite sure what his father would do as governor. They thought and thought about the question and finally Robert, age 8, said, 'He'll make more money, I guess.' "

3/1/72

Dealing with American Express is as bad as it was a decade ago. I suppose almost everybody who has one of their credit cards has a story that can top this one. Anyway . . .

So long ago I've forgotten when, I asked for one of their cards in my wife's name. It came—but on my account number, so that all her charges came to the office and each month had to be separated from mine, because none of hers had anything to do with business and some of mine did. So, well over a year ago, I asked for one in her name at our home address. Months went by. Bills, papers, and tempers flew. Finally, some weeks ago there came a form referring to the application and asking us to check off references for her in terms of trust officer, banker, broker, accountant, attorney, and gad knows what all.

Then, lo and behold, what do I find in my monthly credit-card statement from American Express recently? A beautifully printed flier entitled "Here Are 8 Good Reasons to Give Your Wife an American Express Money Card (In Her Own Name)."

Subsequently she received, in virtually the same mail, a letter stating that my earlier application for her was "canceled" unless she sent in her accountant's name, and another envelope enclosing her American Express card as per application on "8 Good Reasons to Give Your Wife One"!

So, I've told my wife and kids and people here—if your time means anything to you (or this company), use your American Express credit card only as a last resort, only if they won't take anything else, including money.

8/1/73

In August I commented about the rejection of my application for an American Express card for my wife arriving in the same mail as an American Express credit card in her name sent in response to a direct-mail invitation.

On August 7 an American Express card sales manager called and said their records showed they had never issued her a card; a week later, the same gentleman in a very nice letter wrote that ". . . I am enclosing an application for Mrs. Forbes to complete. If and when application is returned to my office, I will have it processed through our special handling unit in New York (this service is available to anyone needing a credit card immediately) and she should have her card within 14 days."

In the same mail a very nice letter from a senior vice-president explained in some detail why my request for her card had been rejected (in essence, "inadequate information") and hers had been accepted ("the type of card issued depends on the type of application received").

Meantime, one of their stockholders had written them querying them about the *Forbes* article, and a different vice-president replied: "Although Mr. Forbes has made public comment, understandably we are not in a position to reveal information that I am sure is presumed to be confidential by both Mr. and Mrs. Forbes. The article is one-sided and does omit pertinent information."

Now, how do you like that for implications? I dropped him a note explaining that neither of us can conceive of anything in the files of American Express that we would consider confidential—and that another vice-president had just nicely explained they didn't have *enough* information.

I don't know what Phase 3 of this Continuing Saga will bring, but if my wife uses the card that the sales manager says she hasn't got, maybe they won't know where to send the bills.

10/1/73

On the occasion of my forty-ninth birthday, there was a telephone call from mother.

In the course of the conversation, this lovely lady said, "You were the most beautiful baby."

I couldn't help chuckling as I thought what a compliment that would be in the language of her grandchildren—with a slight change in one word and the addition of a comma.

"You are the most beautiful, baby."

What a difference the tense makes.

9/15/68

Our teen-age daughter floored me with a couple of observations when I recently met her and my wife as they flew back from vacation.

"Pop, you should have seen how the Oldy Goldies behaved on the plane!"

Like you, I hadn't a clue as to what she meant by an Oldy Goldy and on asking was told, "You know, old businessmen like you."

And what had they done that was drawing her rebuke?

"Boy, the way their eyes travel every time these stewardesses come out in some new outfit.

"My husband is never going to be allowed to fly in an airplane!"

9/15/68

Gadzooks! In less than a week I'll be fifty years old.

All through the teens and the twenties and even well into the thirties, I considered the fifties and the sixties and the seventies as virtually one and the same—ancient.

For yours truly there's cold comfort in that old saw about a person being only as old as he feels. The fact is I ache all over. While the immediate reason has nothing to do with aging, aging is really the reason for these current aches. . . . Having thoroughly enjoyed motorcycle-trail biking with a couple of my sons summertimes in remote rocky mountains, we "graduated" to heavier street cycles. Last Fourth of July I took a 1,100-mile spin from New York to Quebec and back. En route, through dumbness compounded by carelessness, I made part of the trip on my face when my cycle slid in one direction and I in another. No serious results, except a shattered ego and lingering assorted hurts, pains, and bruises.

(Please, dear sensible reader, refrain from telling this gray-haired, saddened old hulk to act his age.)

One other piece of dramatic evidence that, no matter what one thinks or feels, there is a difference between fifty and twenty. . . . As a senior in the winter of 1941, I won my letter on the Princeton gym team—you know, bulging biceps and taut pectorals and washboard stomach muscles.

Thirty years later all this evidence of youth and vigor has simply turned fatter and saggier than would be the case for those more wise, who refrained from the dangers of exercise.

I guess what people call the dignity of age must be two or three decades ahead. Right now I am only aware of some self-inflicted indignities involved on the way.

8/15/69

Concerning my editorial lament at reaching the age of fifty, one friend suggested: "Don't complain.

"Think of the alternative."

9/15/69

Conclusion

Time—Run on if you must
but, please don't run out.
Take yours, time.
Or, to put it another way,
Stop the world.
I don't want to get off.

8/15/72

Index

A Note About the Author

Malcolm S. Forbes was born in Englewood, New Jersey, in 1919. He was graduated from Princeton University in 1941 and published newspapers in Ohio until the next year, when he was inducted into the Army. As a staff sergeant in Europe, he was awarded the Bronze Star and the Purple Heart. After the war he joined *Forbes* magazine, the business publication founded by his father. Upon the latter's death in 1954 he became editor and publisher of the magazine, presiding over its period of great growth to the current semi-monthly circulation of 625,000. Politically active, he was a New Jersey state senator from 1952 to 1958 and Republican candidate for governor in 1957. Among his extracurricular interests are riding motorcycles and flying balloons. In 1973 he became the first to cross the United States in a hot-air balloon, breaking six world records. Mr. Forbes and his wife have five children, and live in Far Hills, New Jersey.

A Note on the Type

This book was set in Monticello, a Linotype revival of the original Roman No. 1 cut by Archibald Binny and cast in 1796 by the Philadelphia type foundry Binny & Ronaldson. The face was named Monticello in honor of its use in the monumental fifty-volume *Papers of Thomas Jefferson*, published by Princeton University Press. Monticello is a transitional type design, embodying certain features of Bulmer and Baskerville, but it is a distinguished face in its own right.

This book was composed, printed, and bound by The Haddon Craftsmen, Inc., Scranton, Pennsylvania.

The typography and binding design are by Earl Tidwell.